STECK-VAUGHN

PHONICS

BOOK A

Author

Barbara K. York

Reviewers

Mary Goosby, Principal
George Pullman Elementary School
School District 10
Chicago, Illinois

Mary Jane Hale, Teacher
Sandpiper Shores Elementary School
Boca Raton, Florida

Cathy Hembree, Reading Specialist
Alta Vista Elementary School
Phoenix, Arizona

Joel Hillman, Director of Communication Arts
Community School District 9
New York, New York

Marsha Solana, Assistant Superintendent of Curriculum
Diocese of Austin
Austin, Texas

STECK-VAUGHN
COMPANY
ELEMENTARY • SECONDARY • ADULT • LIBRARY

About the Author
Barbara K. York

Barbara York's unique blend of many years' experience as an elementary teacher, textbook editor, and author provide her with perspective and insight into children and how they learn to read. She has worked in cooperation with Publications Division of the Bank Street College of Education, the Educational Research Council of America, and several educational publishers. She is a member of the Development Council of the College of Education, Texas A & M University. She is the author of an adult reading series and has been a member of the author team of a major reading series. Her master's degree is from Northeastern University in Boston, and her bachelor's degree is from the University of Massachusetts.

Acknowledgments

Grateful acknowledgment is made to the following authors, agents, and publishers for the use of copyrighted materials:

"Brooms" by Dorothy Aldis reprinted by permission of G. P. Putnam's Sons from EVERYTHING AND ANYTHING, copyright 1925-1927, copyright renewed © 1953-1955 by Dorothy Aldis.

Bobbi Katz for "Morning Song" from POEMS FOR SMALL FRIENDS by Bobbi Katz. Copyright © Random House, 1989. Used with permission of Bobbi Katz.

"Notice" from ONE AT A TIME by David McCord. Copyright © 1952 by David McCord. By permission of Little, Brown and Company.

Photography

Cover Photography: Cooke Photographics
Henry Ausloos/Animals, Animals,
Elizabeth Billhardt/The Image Bank
Cindi Ellis
Melissa Hayes English/Photo Researchers, Inc.
Kenneth W. Fink/Photo Researchers, Inc.
Guy Gillette/Photo Researchers, Inc.
P. W. Grace/Photo Researchers, Inc.
D. P. Hershkowitz/Bruce Coleman, Inc.
Walter Hodge/Peter Arnold
Jacana/The Image Bank
Lou Jones/The Image Bank
Ken Lax
Hans Pfletschinger/Peter Arnold
Leonard Lee Rue III/Photo Researchers, Inc.
Ted Russell/The Image Bank
Paul Shabroom/Photo Researchers, Inc.
Kim Taylor/Bruce Coleman, Inc.

Illustration

Ben Anglin
Rhonda Childress
Holly Cooper
Creston Ely
David Griffin
Mike Krone
Lynn McClain
Lyle Miller
Larry Nolte
T. K. Riddle
Lou Vaccaro
Joe Veno

Staff

Executive Editor: Wendy Whitnah
Project Editor: Melissa Blackwell Burke
Design Manager: Pamela Heaney

1995 EDITION   **ISBN 0-8114-6521-7**

4 5 6 7 8 9 PO 99 98 97 96 95

CONTENTS

Unit 1   **Auditory and Visual Discrimination, Letter Recognition**

Auditory Discrimination 1
Visual Discrimination 5
Letter Recognition: *Aa-Zz* 7
Assessment 27

Unit 2   **Consonants and Short Vowels**

Initial Consonants *m, d, f,* and *g* 29
Final Consonants *m, d, f,* and *g* 37
Short Vowel *a* 39
Read a Story: Apply Short Vowel *a* To Decode Words in Context 47
Read a Poem: "Notice" by David McCord 49
Assessment 51
Initial Consonants *b, t, s,* and *w* 53
Final Consonants *b, t,* and *s* 61
Short Vowel *o* 63
Read a Story: Apply Short Vowel *o* To Decode Words in Context 73
Assessment: *b, t, s, w,* and *o* 75
Initial Consonants *k, j, p,* and *n* 77
Final Consonants *k, p,* and *n* 85
Short Vowel *i* 87
Read a Story: Apply Short Vowel *i* To Decode Words in Context 97
Read a Poem: "Mix a Pancake" by Christina Rossetti 99
Assessment 101
Initial Consonants *c, h, l,* and *r* 103
Short Vowel *u* 111
Read a Story: Apply Short Vowel *u* To Decode Words in Context 121
Read a Poem: "The Way They Scrub" by A. B. Ross 123
Assessment 125
Initial Consonants *v, y, z,* and *qu* 127
Final Consonants *x, l,* and *v* 134
Short Vowel *e* 137
Medial Consonants *g, l,* and *m* 147
Read a Story: Apply Short Vowel *e* To Decode Words in Context 151
Make a Book 153
Assessment 155

Unit 3   Long Vowels

Long Vowel *a* 157
Read a Story: Apply Long Vowel *a* To Decode Words in Context 163
Long Vowel *i* 165
Read a Story: Apply Long Vowel *i* To Decode Words in Context 171
Long Vowel *o* 173
Read a Story: Apply Long Vowel *o* To Decode Words in Context 179
Long Vowel *u* 181
Read a Story: Apply Long Vowel *u* To Decode Words in Context 187
Long Vowel *e* 189
Read a Story: Apply Long Vowel *e* To Decode Words in Context 195
Final *y* as a Vowel 197
Read a Poem: "Old King Cole," Nursery Rhyme 203
Make a Book 205
Assessment 207

Unit 4   Consonant Blends and Digraphs

Initial Blends with *s, tw* 209
Initial Blends with *r* 213
Initial Blends with *l* 217
Initial Digraphs *ch* and *wh* 221
Initial Digraphs *sh* and *th* 223
Final Digraphs *ch* and *th* 225
Final Digraphs *sh* and *ck* 226
Final Digraphs *ng* and *nk* 227
Read a Story: Apply Consonant Blends and Digraphs
   To Decode Words in Context 233
Read a Poem: "Brooms" by Dorothy Aldis 235
Assessment 237

Unit 5   Plurals, Inflectional Endings, Contractions, and Compounds

Plurals 239
Inflectional Endings 243
Read a Story: Apply Plurals and Inflectional Endings
   To Decode Words in Context 247
Contractions 249
Compounds 251
Read a Poem: "Morning Song" by Bobbi Katz 253
Make a Book 255
Assessment 257
Final Assessment 259

Name each picture. Listen to the first sound.
Draw a line to match the picture names that
begin with the same sound.

Name _____

UNIT 1: Auditory Discrimination of Initial Consonant Sounds 1

Name the first picture in each row. Listen to the beginning sound. Name the other pictures in the row. Color the ones that begin with the same sound as the first picture name.

Name each picture. Draw lines to match the picture names that rhyme.

Name _____

UNIT 1: Auditory Discrimination; Rhyme 3

Say each picture name. Find the picture names that rhyme. Circle the pictures.

Look at the first letter in each row.
Circle the same letter each time you
see it in the row.

D	B	(D)	O	(D)	(D)
R	R	R	B	R	P
T	L	T	T	I	T
g	g	g	j	g	q
m	u	m	n	m	m
f	l	f	f	f	t

Name _____

Look at the first word in each row.
Circle the same word each time you
see it in the row.

go	no	go	so	go
at	at	an	at	am
get	jet	pet	get	get
dog	log	got	dog	dog
bell	bell	doll	bet	bell
can	cat	can	can	cap
eat	eat	eel	eat	tea

Trace and write the letters. Then find
and circle each capital **A** and small **a**.
Do the same for **B** and **b** below.

A A A

a a a

A	O	A	C	A	a	o	c	a	a	g

at	can	ran	Ann	Al	and

B B B

b b b

B	A	B	P	B	b	g	b	a	a	b

bat	cab	Bob	big	tab

Name _____

UNIT 1: Visual Recognition of Letters Aa, Bb   **7**

Trace and write the letters. Then find
and circle each capital **C** and small **c**.
Do the same for **D** and **d** below.

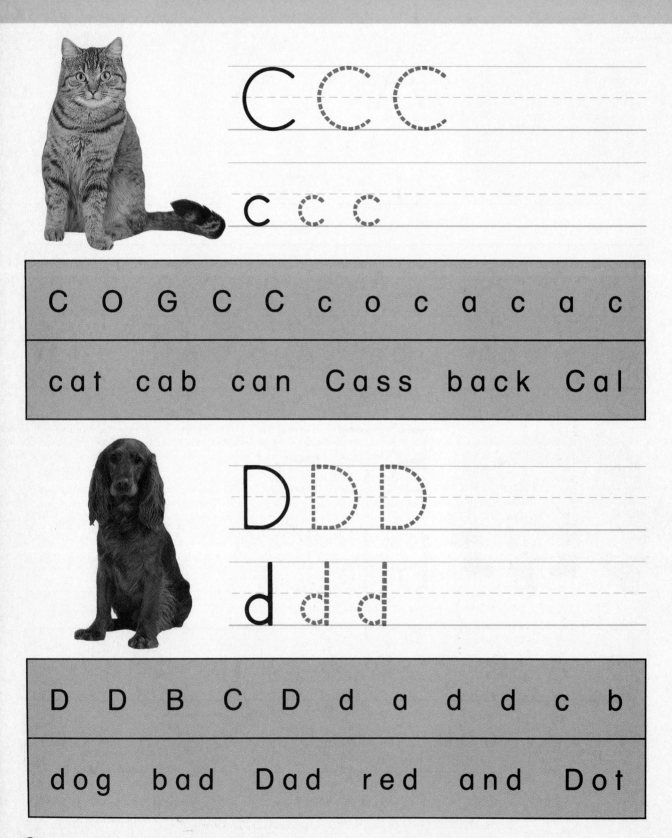

C C C C

c c c c

| C | O | G | C | C | c | o | c | a | c | a | c |

cat   cab   can   Cass   back   Cal

D D D D

d d d d

| D | D | B | C | D | d | a | d | d | c | b |

dog   bad   Dad   red   and   Dot

Draw lines to match the capital and
small letters.
At the bottom, circle the letters in the
row that match the red letter.

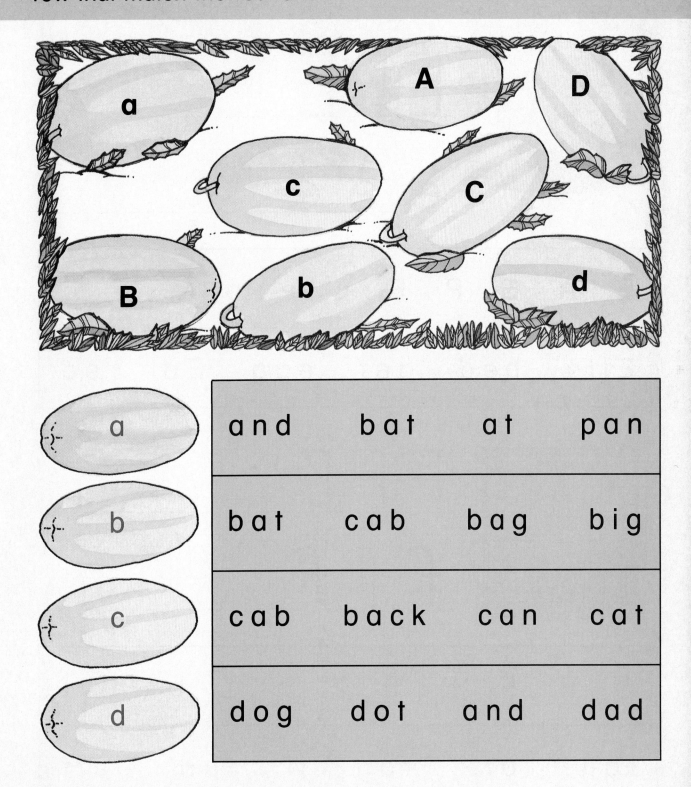

a	and	bat	at	pan
b	bat	cab	bag	big
c	cab	back	can	cat
d	dog	dot	and	dad

Name _____

Trace and write the letters. Then find
and circle each capital **E** and small **e**.
Do the same for **F** and **f** below.

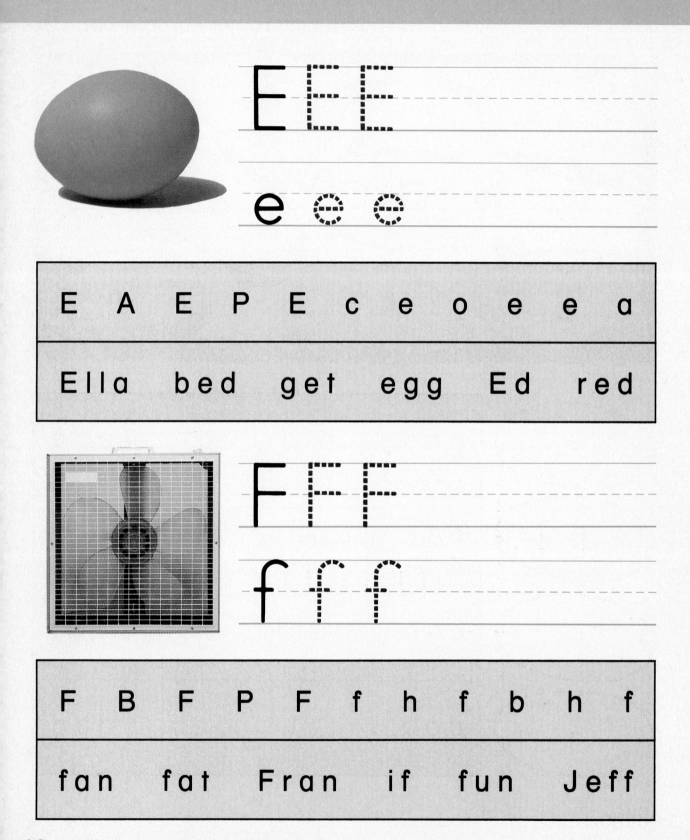

E E E

e e e

| E | A | E | P | E | c | e | o | e | e | a |

Ella   bed   get   egg   Ed   red

F F F

f f f

| F | B | F | P | F | f | h | f | b | h | f |

fan   fat   Fran   if   fun   Jeff

Trace and write the letters. Then find
and circle each capital **G** and small **g.**
Do the same for **H** and **h** below.

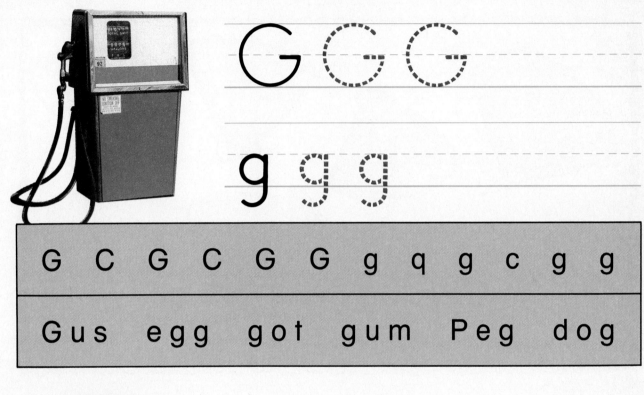

G	C	G	C	G	G	g	q	g	c	g	g

Gus	egg	got	gum	Peg	dog

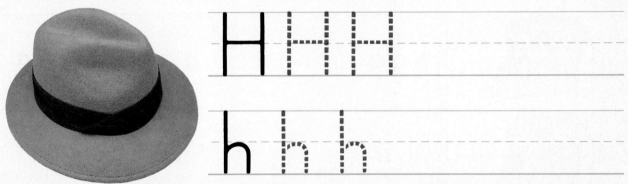

H	E	H	E	H	H	h	b	h	d	h	h

Hal	had	fish	he	Helen	hot

Name _____

Draw lines to match the capital and small letters.
At the bottom, circle the letters in the row that match the red letter.

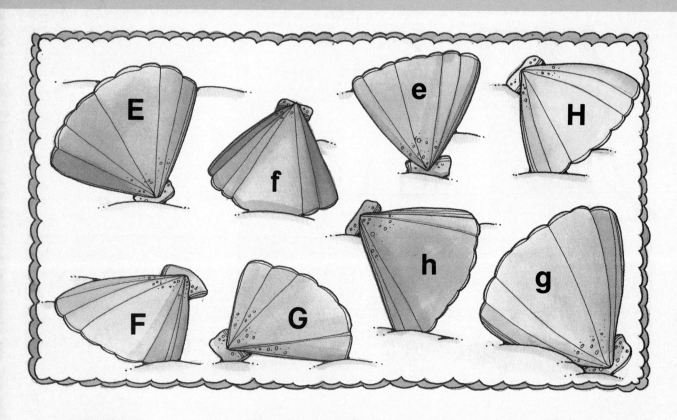

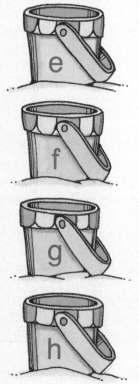

egg	red	bed	Peg
fun	if	fan	Jeff
gum	big	dog	egg
ash	hat	hot	ham

Trace and write the letters. Then find
and circle each capital **I** and small **i**.
Do the same for **J** and **j** below.

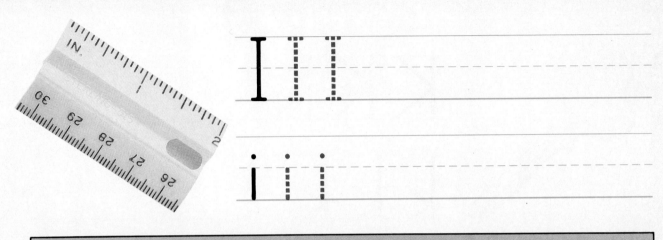

| I | E | I | T | I | i | j | h | i | i | i |

in   Inez   it   India   if   did

| J | I | J | F | T | J | j | i | j | j | j |

Jan   jog   Jed   jam   job   jet

Name _____

UNIT 1: Visual Recognition of Letters Ii, Jj

Trace and write the letters. Then find
and circle each capital **K** and small **k**.
Do the same for **L** and **l** below.

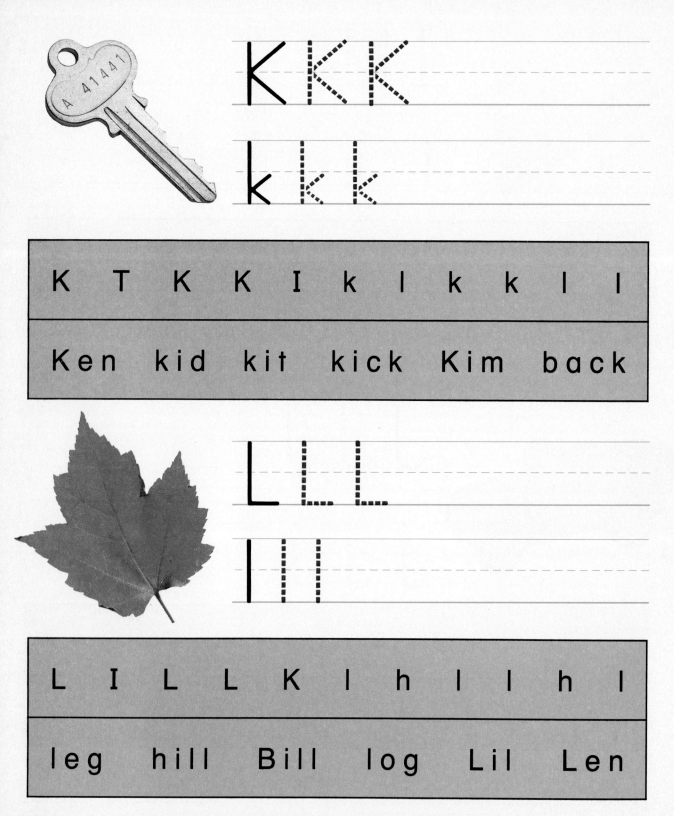

K K K

k k k

K T K K I k l k k l l

Ken   kid   kit   kick   Kim   back

L L L

l l l

L I L L K l h l l h l

leg   hill   Bill   log   Lil   Len

Draw lines to match the capital and small letters.
At the bottom, circle the letters in the row that match the red letter.

in	did	it	if
jam	job	jet	jog
kid	kit	back	kick
log	hill	leg	milk

Name _____

UNIT 1: Review Visual Recognition of Letters I-L

15

Trace and write the letters. Then find
and circle each capital **M** and small **m.**
Do the same for **N** and **n** below.

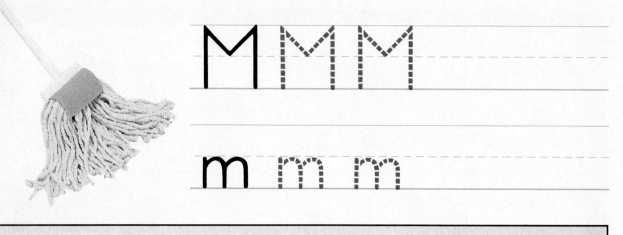

M	N	M	W	M	m	m	u	n	u	m

man	met	mop	Mom	ham	Matt

N	N	M	N	N	n	u	n	u	n	m

not	Ned	nun	nap	net	Nan

Trace and write the letters. Then find
and circle each capital **O** and small **o**.
Do the same for **P** and **p** below.

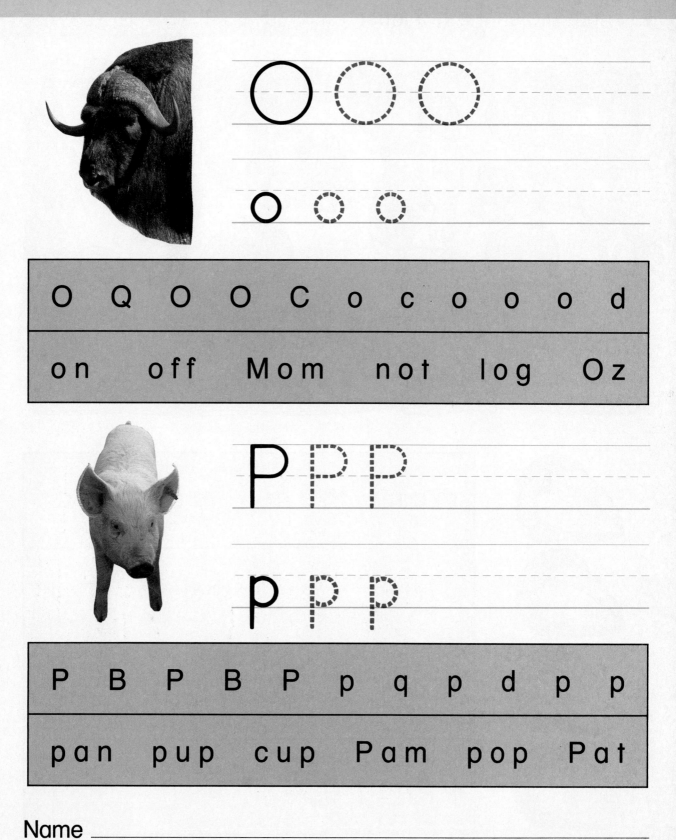

O O O

o o o

O   Q   O   O   C   o   c   o   o   o   d

on   off   Mom   not   log   Oz

P P P

p p p

P   B   P   B   P   p   q   p   d   p   p

pan   pup   cup   Pam   pop   Pat

Name _____

Draw lines to match the capital and
small letters.
At the bottom, circle the letters in the
row that match the red letter.

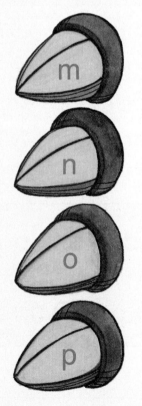

man	ham	met	mat
not	net	nun	fun
mom	not	on	off
pan	pat	cup	pop

Trace and write the letters. Then find
and circle each capital **Q** and small **q.**
Do the same for **R** and **r** below.

Q   Q   Q

q   q   q

Q	O	Q	C	Q	q	g	q	q	p	q

quack   quit   quiz   Quin   equal

R   R   R

r   r   r

R	P	R	D	R	r	r	n	r	u	r

ran   Rob   red   rug   car   Ron

Name _____

UNIT 1: Visual Recognition of Letters Qq, Rr   19

Trace and write the letters. Then find
and circle each capital **S** and small **s**.
Do the same for **T** and **t** below.

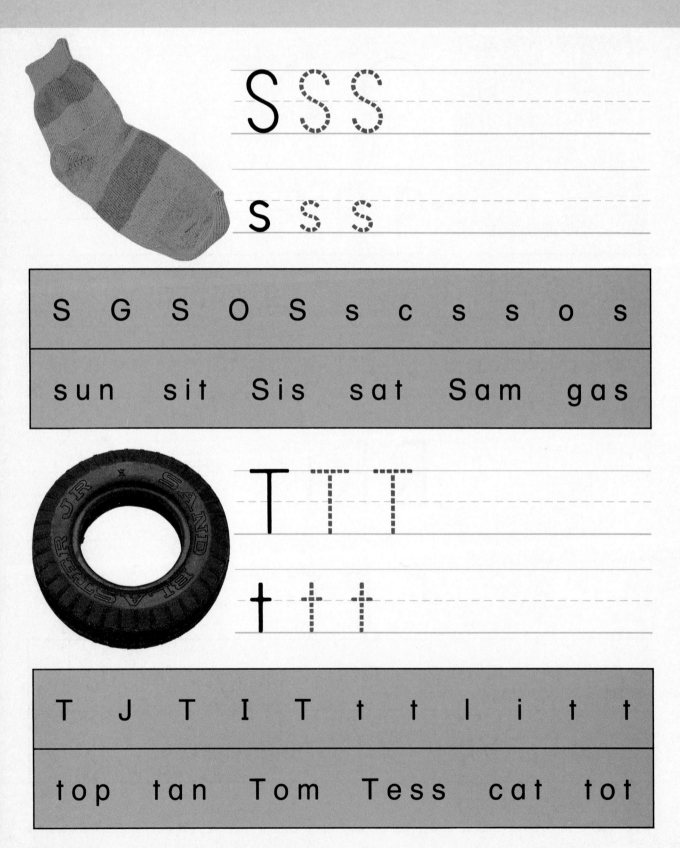

S S S

s s s

| S | G | S | O | S | s | c | s | s | o | s |

| sun | sit | Sis | sat | Sam | gas |

T T T

t t t

| T | J | T | I | T | t | t | l | i | t | t |

| top | tan | Tom | Tess | cat | tot |

Draw lines to match the capital and small letters.

At the bottom, circle the letters in the row that match the red letter.

quack	quit	quiz	squat
rat	your	red	run
sun	sis	gas	sat
tot	tan	top	cat

Name _____

Trace and write the letters. Then find
and circle each capital **U** and small **u.**
Do the same for **V** and **v** below.

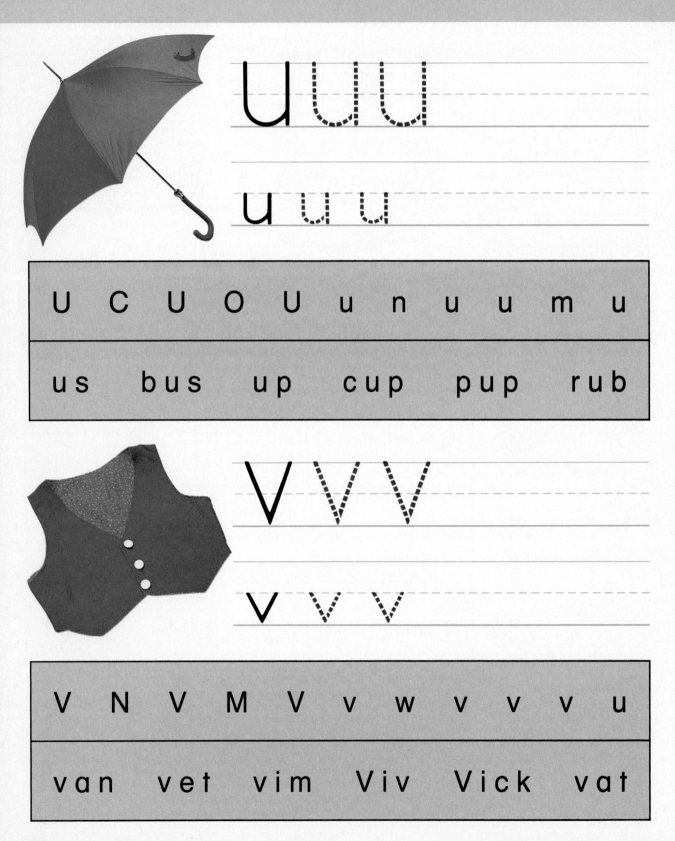

u u u

u u u

| U | C | U | O | U | u | n | u | u | m | u |

us   bus   up   cup   pup   rub

V V V

V V V

| V | N | V | M | V | v | w | v | v | v | u |

van   vet   vim   Viv   Vick   vat

Trace and write the letters. Then find
and circle each capital **W** and small **w.**
Do the same for **X** and **x** below.

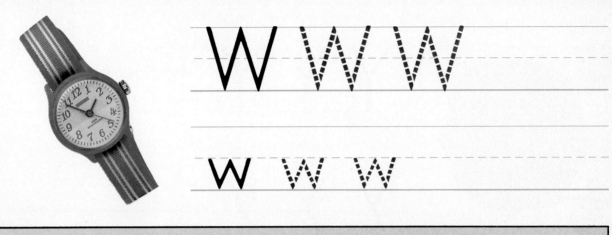

W W W

w w w

| W | M | W | N | W | w | v | v | w | w | w |

| Ward | new | wig | wet | we | Will |

X X X

x x x

| X | A | X | V | X | x | w | x | v | x | x |

| ax | six | fox | mix | Rex | box |

Name _____

Trace and write the letters. Then find
and circle each capital **Y** and small **y.**
Do the same for **Z** and **z** below.

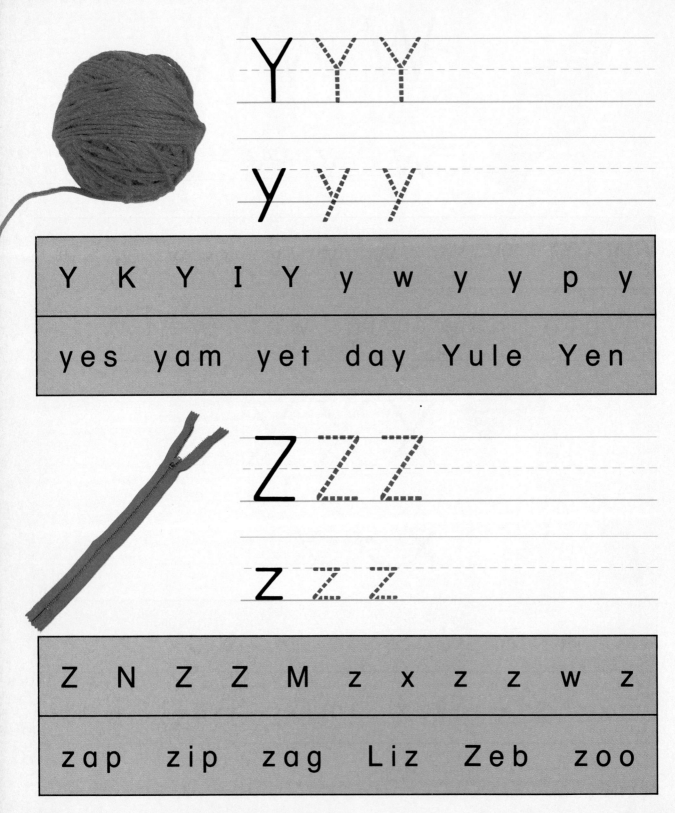

Y   K   Y   I   Y   y   w   y   y   p   y

yes   yam   yet   day   Yule   Yen

Z   N   Z   Z   M   z   x   z   z   w   z

zap   zip   zag   Liz   Zeb   zoo

Draw lines to match the capital and small letters.

At the bottom, circle the letters in the row that match the red letter.

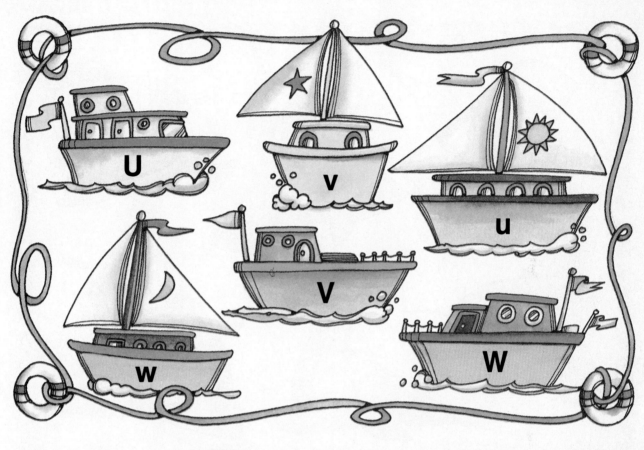

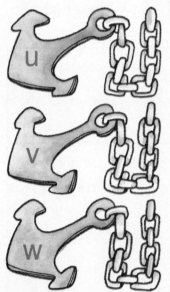

up	cup	mug	fun
van	vet	vat	love
will	two	was	wet

Name _____

UNIT 1: Review Visual Recognition of Letters U-W   25

Draw lines to match the capital and small letters.
At the bottom, circle the letters in the row that match the red letter.

box	fix	ax	six
toy	yes	you	yam
zip	zap	zoo	Oz

Listen to your teacher.
Circle the letter that your teacher says.

	1	2	3
🍎	l t b	F D O	v w m
kite	I T L	j q p	G O C
backpack	K L H	n w x	P R B
umbrella	A M W	v l i	c a o
heart	K P T	V M W	F I E
cup	K G H	c o s	G O U
star	Q C G	d p b	Z J T
cap	r n m	Z Y X	x w v
leaf	a c o	n u w	T L I

Name _____

Listen to your teacher.
Circle the letter that your teacher says.

	1	2	3
	G O Q	L X S	F B H
	V M W	G O P	j w n
	Z X Y	t f h	a e o
	s f d	W X Z	W N X
	i u m	i w x	a c o
	n w m	S G C	b h f
	q g p	x h v	T F P
	m z v	O G C	M W N
	y g q	e p k	a g w

UNIT 1: Assess Visual Recognition of Letters A-Z
Note: See Teacher's Edition for test script.

Mop begins with the **m** sound.
Name each picture and listen to the first
sound. Color the ones that begin with
the **m** sound.

m

Name

Write **m** if the picture name begins with the **m** sound.

m

m

Dog begins with the **d** sound. Name each picture and listen to the first sound. Color the ones that begin with the **d** sound.

d

Write **d** if the picture name begins with the **d** sound.

Fan begins with the **f** sound.
Name each picture and listen to the first sound. Color the ones that begin with the **f** sound.

f

Name _____

Write **f** if the picture name begins with the **f** sound.

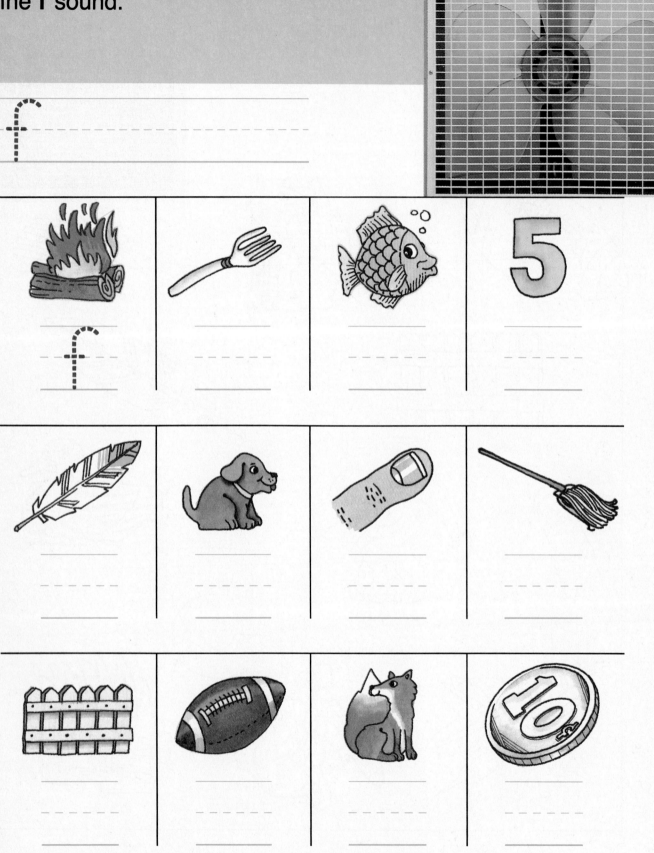

f

f _ _ _ _ _ _ _ _ _ _

_ _ _ _ _ _ _ _ _ _

Gas begins with the **g** sound.
Name each picture and listen to the first
sound. Color the ones that begin with
the **g** sound.

g

SUGARLESS

Name

Write **g** if the picture name begins with the **g** sound.

g

Circle the letter for the **last** sound.
Then write the letter.

 ha**m**   be**d**   lea**f**    lo**g**

f g (d)	m d g	f g d	m d f
d			

m g f	m d f	f g d	m g f

m f g	m d g	m f g	m d f

Name _____

UNIT 2: Final Consonants m, d, f, g **37**

Write the missing letter to complete each word.

ham   dam   fan   log

__as   el_   da_   _an

be_   ru_   ja_   le_

_at   _ig   ba_   _ox

Apple begins with the short **a** sound.
Name the pictures. Color those whose
names begin with the short **a** sound.

Name _____

UNIT 2: Initial Short Vowel a   **39**

Dam has the short **a** sound.
Name the pictures. Color each picture
whose name has the short **a** sound.

dam

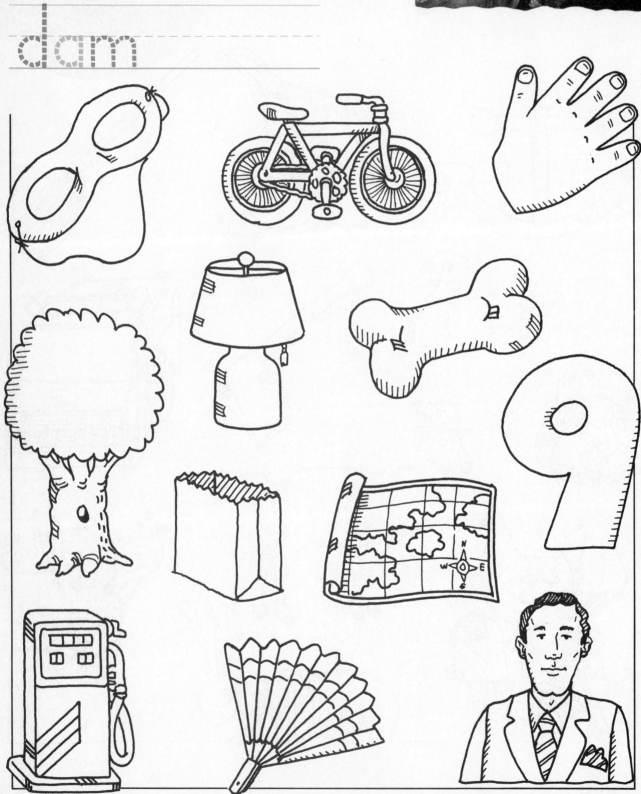

Say each picture name. Write **a** if you hear the short **a** sound.

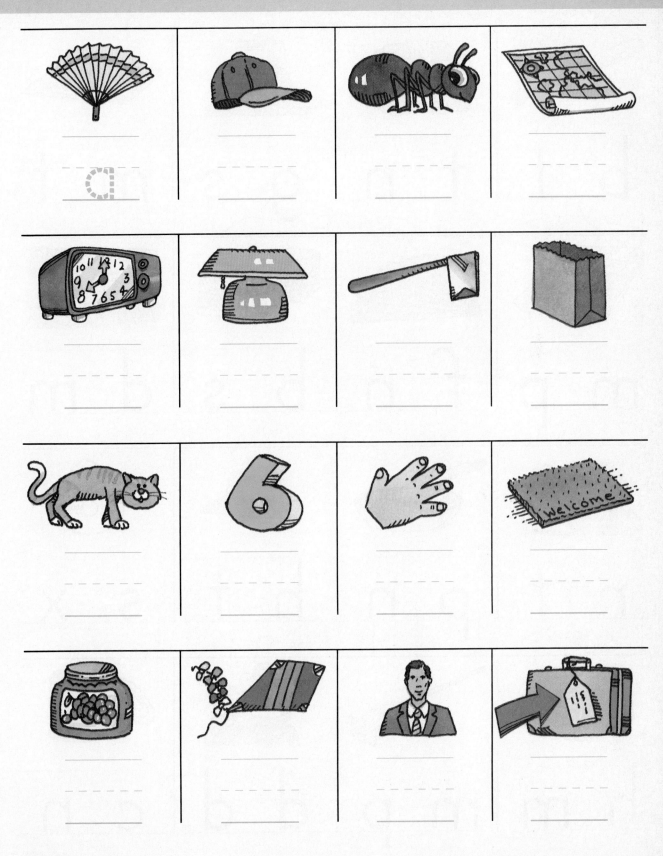

UNIT 2: Short Vowel a   41

Say each picture name. Write **a** if you
hear the short **a** sound.

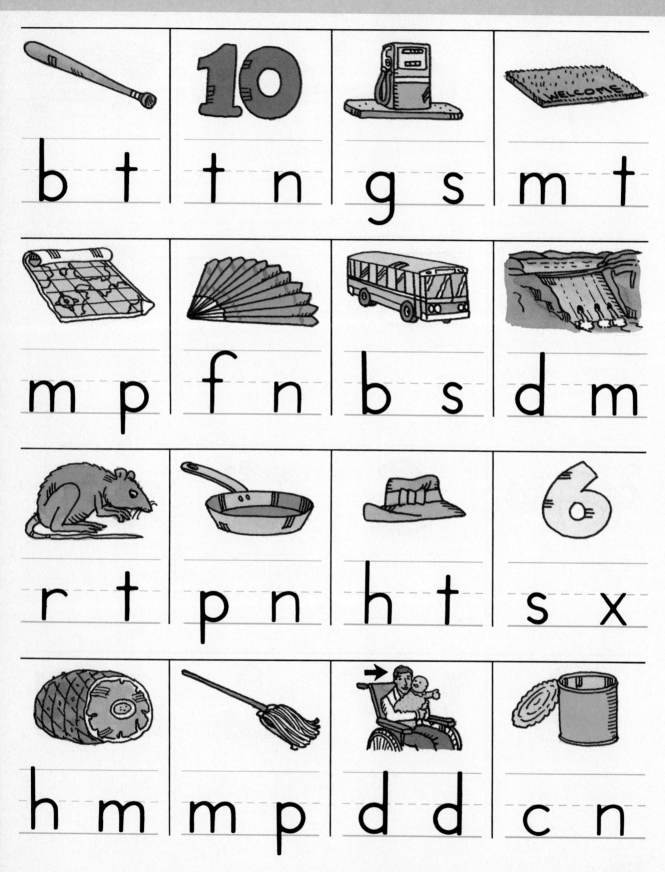

b t   t n   g s   m t

m p   f n   b s   d m

r t   p n   h t   s x

h m   m p   d d   c n

Name the pictures. Color each picture whose name rhymes with the word at the beginning of the row.

fan			
dam			
mat			
map			
add			

Name _____

Look at the letter in the box.
Draw a line from the letter to
the picture whose name
begins with the letter.

Listen to the **first** sound in each picture name. Find that letter on a crayon. Use your crayons to make each fish the right color.

m d a f g

Name _____

UNIT 2: Review Initial m, d, f, g, a   45

Name the picture. Circle the picture name. Write the name.

(mat)	had	fan
cat	dad	pan
rat	fad	man

mat

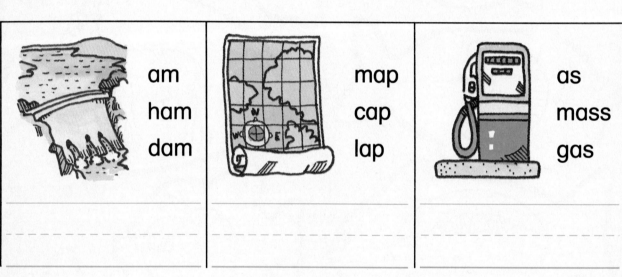

am	map	as
ham	cap	mass
dam	lap	gas

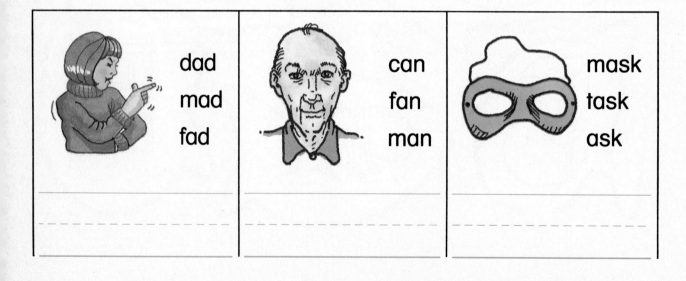

dad	can	mask
mad	fan	task
fad	man	ask

Read the story. Then read the
question. Write the answer in a
complete sentence. Color the picture.

Al

Al is mad.
Al has no gas.

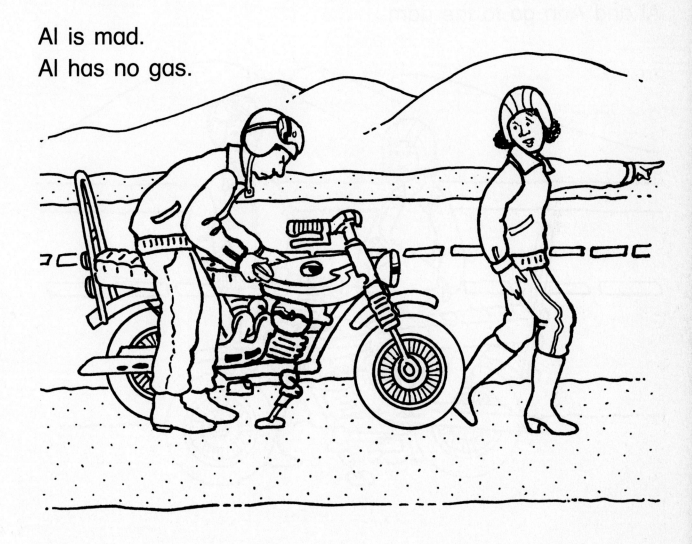

Who is mad?

_____

_____

_____

Name _____

Read more of the story. Then read the question. Write the answer in a complete sentence. Color the picture.

Ann adds gas for Al.
Al and Ann go to the dam.

Who adds gas?

_____

_____

Notice

I have a dog,
I had a cat.
I've got a frog
Inside my hat.

David McCord

Think of something to put in a hat.
Draw a picture of it.

Write about your picture.

Name _____

Say the picture name. Write the letter that stands for the **first** sound.

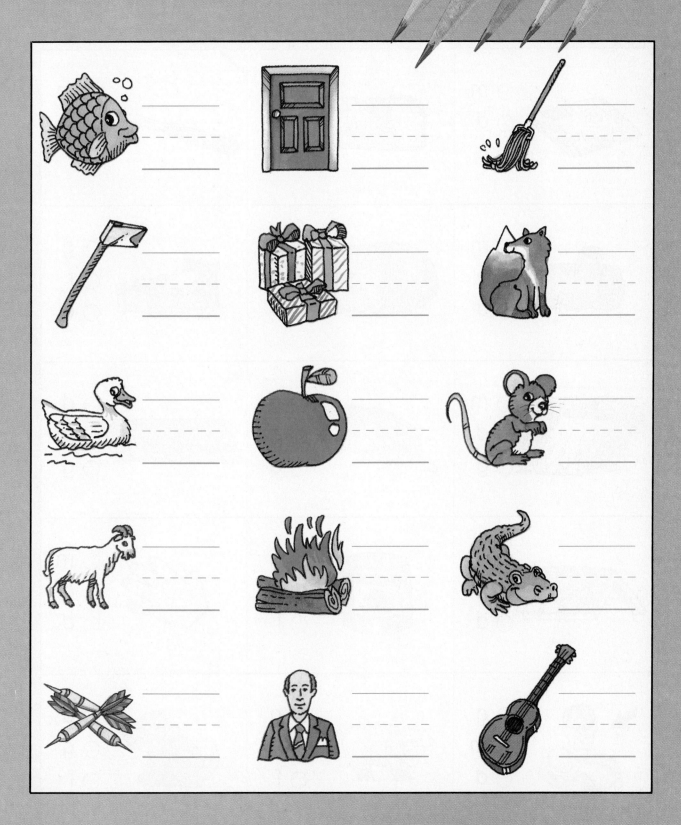

Say the picture name. Fill in the
circle next to the letter for
the **last** sound.

○ m ○ d ○ f	○ g ○ f ○ d	○ m ○ g ○ f
○ m ○ g ○ d	○ d ○ m ○ f	○ g ○ f ○ d
○ m ○ d ○ g	○ m ○ f ○ d	○ d ○ m ○ g
○ g ○ f ○ d	○ g ○ m ○ f	○ m ○ g ○ d
○ g ○ m ○ d	○ g ○ m ○ f	○ d ○ g ○ f

Bus begins with the **b** sound.
Name each picture and listen to the first sound. Color the ones that begin with the **b** sound.

b

Name _____

Write **b** if the picture name begins with the **b** sound.

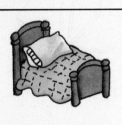

b

 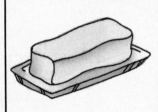  

Tire begins with the **t** sound. Name each picture and listen to the first sound. Color the ones that begin with the **t** sound.

t

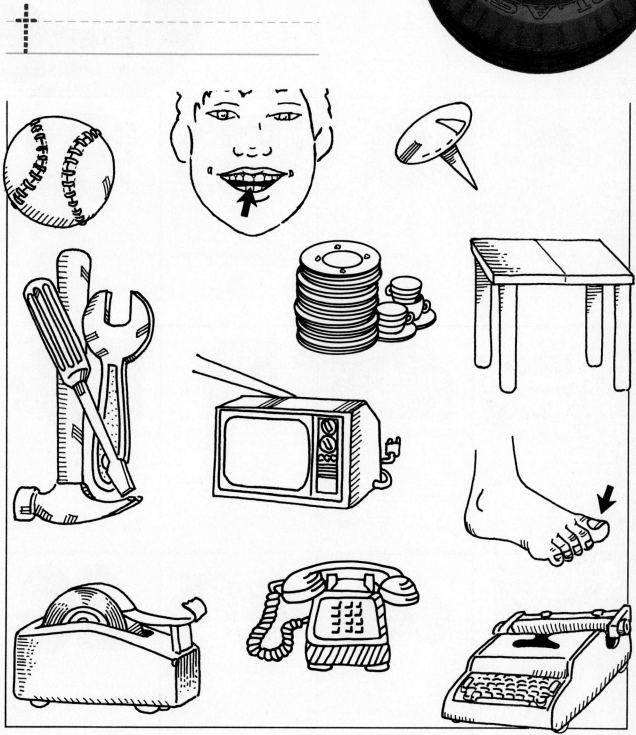

Name _____

Write **t** if the picture name begins with the **t** sound.

t _____

 t |  |  |

 |  |  |

 |  |  |

Sock begins with the **s** sound. Name each picture and listen to the first sound. Color the ones that begin with the **s** sound.

S

Name _____

Write **s** if the picture name begins with the **s** sound.

s _____

Watch begins with the **w** sound.
Name each picture and listen to the first
sound. Color the ones that begin with
the **w** sound.

w

Name

Write **w** if the picture name begins with the **w** sound.

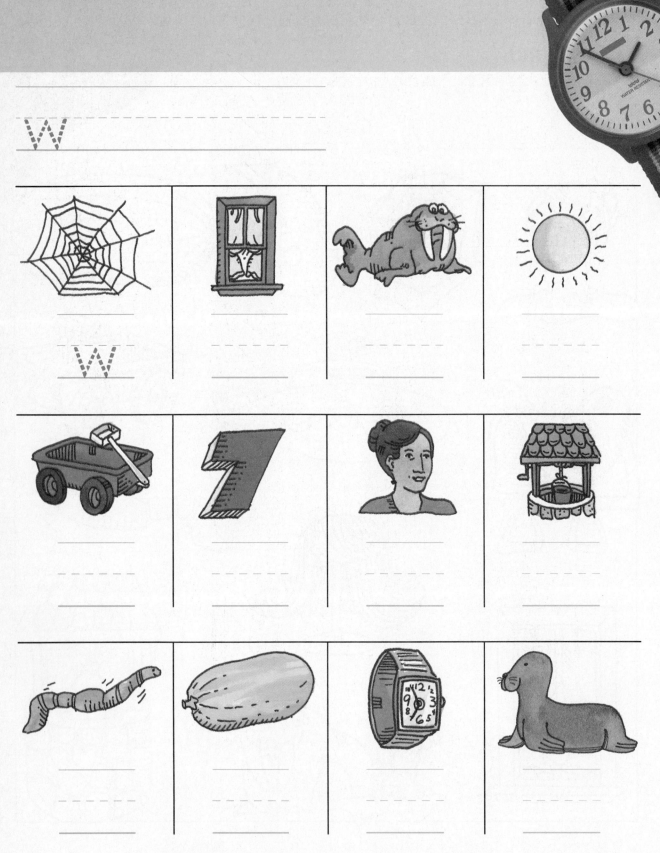

Circle the letter for the **last** sound.
Then write the letter.

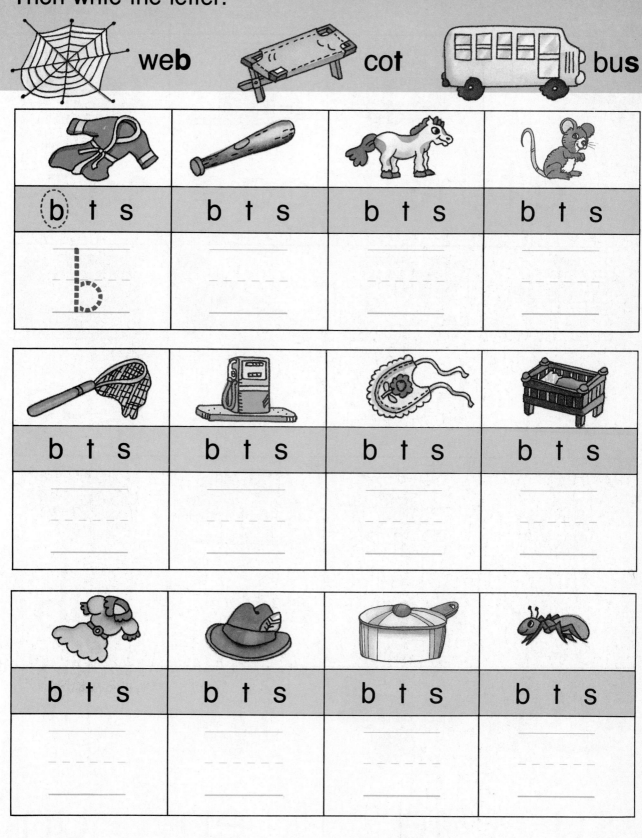

we**b**   co**t**   bu**s**

(b) t s	b t s	b t s	b t s
b			

b t s	b t s	b t s	b t s

b t s	b t s	b t s	b t s

Name _____

UNIT 2: Final Consonants b, t, s   61

Write the missing letter to complete each word.

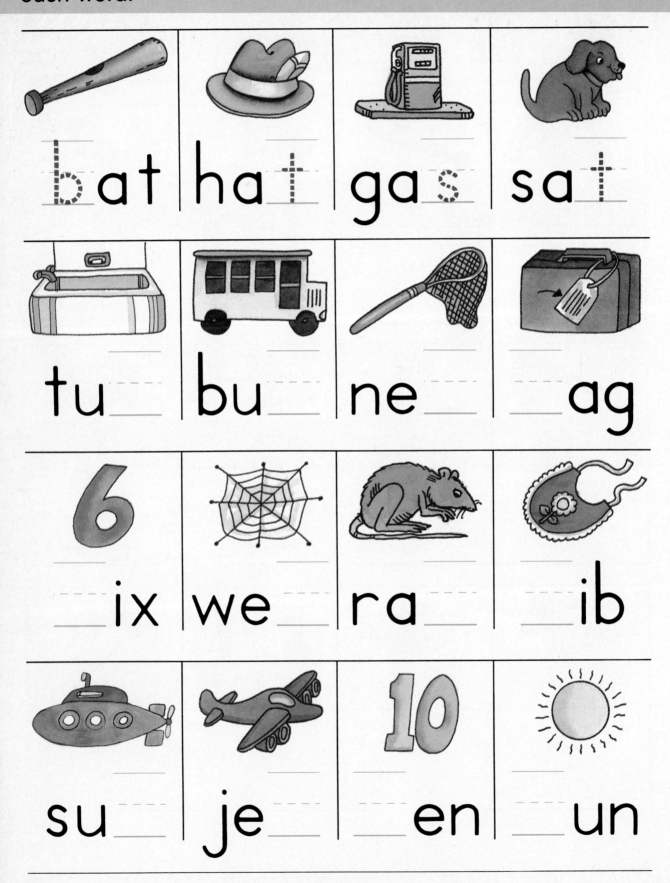

bat hat gas sat

tu_ bu_ ne_ _ag

_ix we_ ra_ _ib

su_ je_ _en _un

Ox begins with the short **o** sound.
Name the pictures. Color those whose
names begin with the short **o** sound.

Name _____

Fox has the short **o** sound.
Name the pictures. Color each picture
whose name has the short **o** sound.

fox

Say each picture name. Write **o** if you hear the short **o** sound.

Say each picture name. Write **o** if you
hear the short **o** sound.

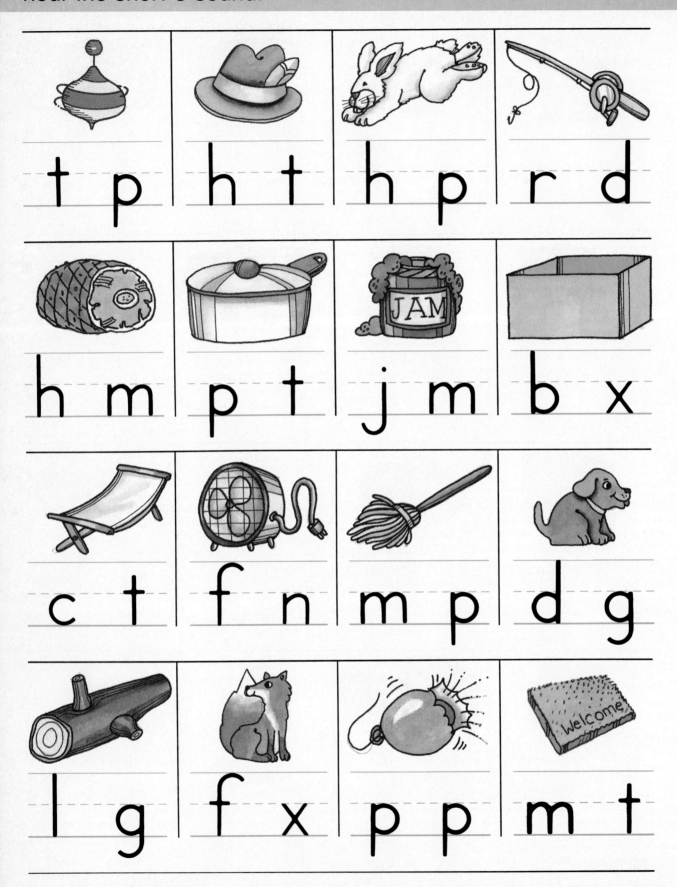

t _ p	h _ t	h _ p	r _ d
h _ m	p _ t	j _ m	b _ x
c _ t	f _ n	m _ p	d _ g
l _ g	f _ x	p _ p	m _ t

Name the pictures. Color each picture whose name rhymes with the word at the beginning of the row.

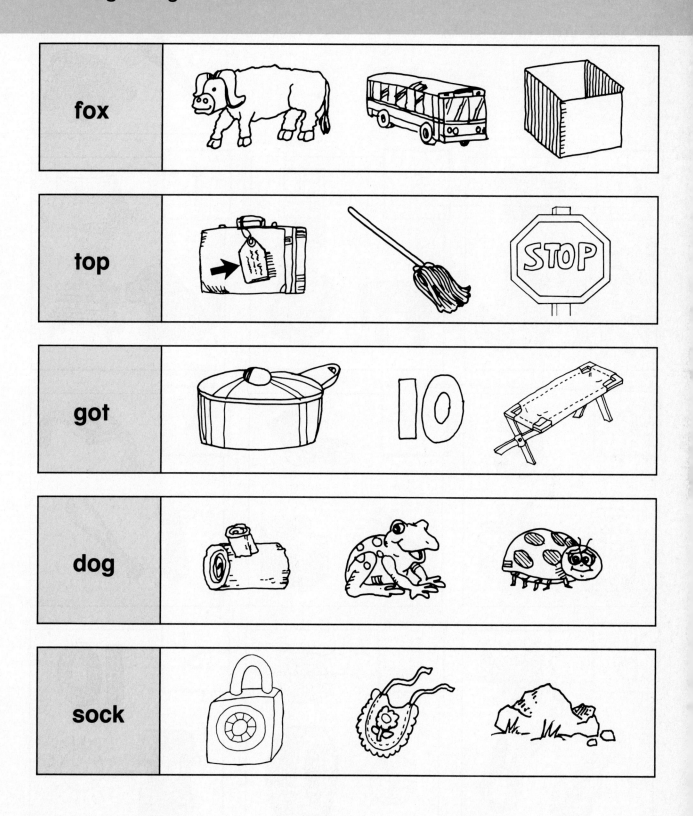

fox			
top			
got			
dog			
sock			

Name _____

UNIT 2: Short Vowel o   **67**

Look at the letter in the box.
Draw a line from the letter to
the picture whose name
begins with the letter.

Listen to the **first** sound in each picture name. Find that letter on a crayon. Use your crayons to make each sock the right color.

b t o s w

Circle the letter for the **vowel** sound.
Then write the letter.

 d a m

 f o x

(a) o	a o	a o	a o
a			

a o	a o	a o	a o

a o	a o	a o	a o

Name the picture. Circle the word.
Write the word.

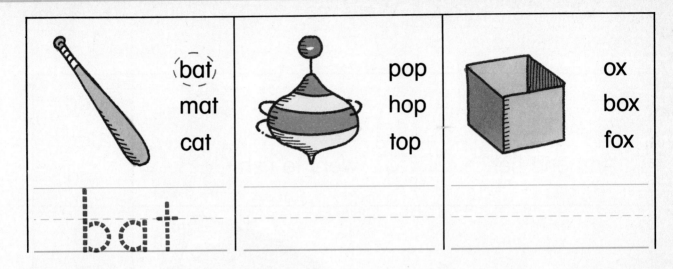

bat
mat
cat

b a t

pop
hop
top

ox
box
fox

back
tack
sack

wag
tag
sag

sock
lock
rock

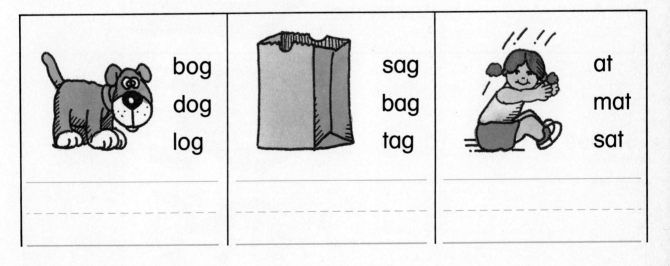

bog
dog
log

sag
bag
tag

at
mat
sat

Name _____

Look at the picture. Then read the sentence. Circle the word that completes the sentence. Write the word on the line.

1. Ann and her _dad_ went to fish.	add dad sad
2. Ann had her _____.	tag sag bag
3. They sat on a _____.	mat bat sat
4. A _____ is on the mat.	got tot dot
5. Dad _____ a fish.	dot got not
6. Ann got a _____ fish.	bat fat sat

Read the story. Then read the sentence.
Write the word that completes the
sentence. Color the picture.

A Job

Bob got a job.
Bob got the mop.
Bob mops for Mom.

_____ got a job.

Name _____

Read more of the story. Then read the
sentence. Write the word that completes
the sentence. Color the picture.

The dog got in.
Mom got mad at the dog.
Bob and Mom mop and mop.

_____ got mad.

Say the picture name. Write the letter that stands for the **first** sound.

Name _____

Say the picture name. Fill in the
circle next to the letter for
the **last** sound.

○ b ○ t ○ s	○ s ○ b ○ t	○ t ○ s ○ b
○ b ○ t ○ s	○ t ○ b ○ s	○ t ○ b ○ s
○ s ○ b ○ t	○ t ○ s ○ b	○ b ○ t ○ s
○ b ○ s ○ t	○ s ○ b ○ t	○ b ○ t ○ s
○ s ○ t ○ b	○ b ○ s ○ t	○ t ○ s ○ b

Key begins with the **k** sound.
Name each picture and listen to the first sound. Color the ones that begin with the **k** sound.

k

Name _____

Write **k** if the picture name begins with
the **k** sound.

k _____

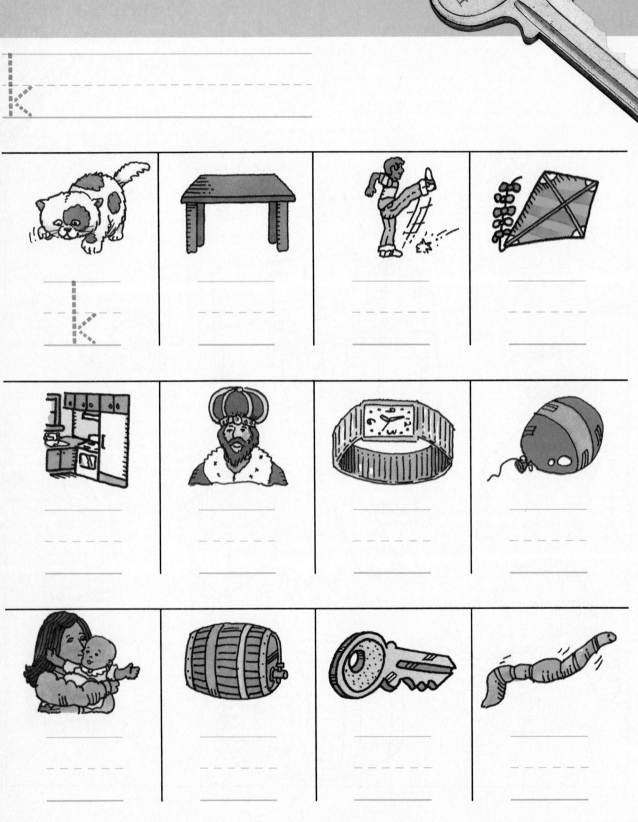

Jeep begins with the **j** sound. Name each picture and listen to the first sound. Color the ones that begin with the **j** sound.

j

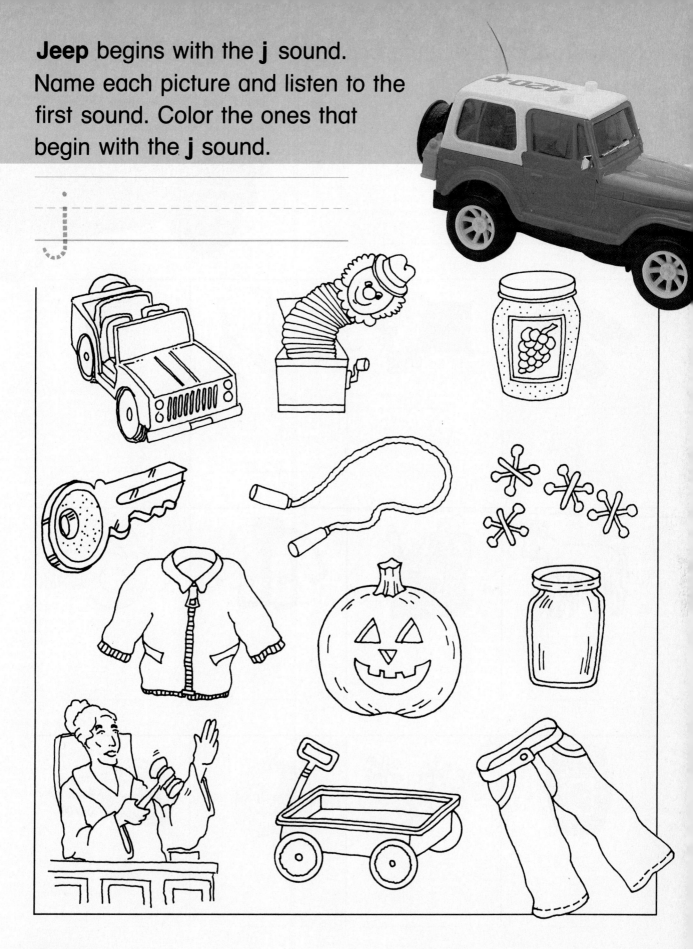

Name _____

Write **j** if the picture name begins with the **j** sound.

j

			j

			6

Pig begins with the **p** sound.
Name each picture and listen to the first
sound. Color the ones that begin with
the **p** sound.

Name _____

Write **p** if the picture name begins with
the **p** sound.

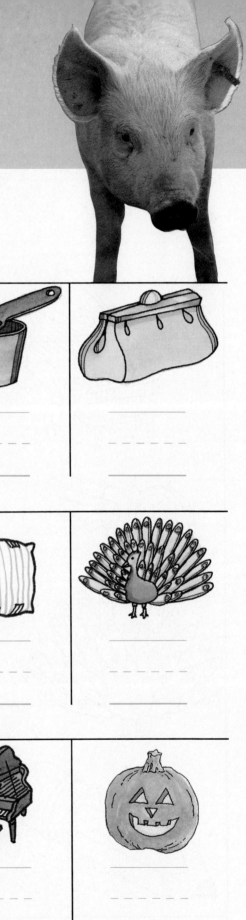

P

p

Nest begins with the **n** sound.
Name each picture and listen to the first
sound. Color the ones that begin with
the **n** sound.

n

Name

Write **n** if the picture name begins with the **n** sound.

n

n

Circle the letter for the **last** sound.
Then write the letter.

for**k**   mo**p**   va**n**

k p (n)	k p n	k p n	k p n
n			

k p n	k p n	k p n	k p n

k p n	k p n	k p n	k p n

Name _____

Write the missing letter to complete each word.

for**k**   **p**et   he**n**   zi**p**

__ et   __ ey   ma __   bea __

__ ig   te __   __ it   __ ut

pa __   lea __   __ in   ma __

Inch begins with the short **i** sound.
Name the pictures. Color those whose
names begin with the short **i** sound.

Name _____

Mitt has the short **i** sound.
Name the pictures. Color each picture
whose name has the short **i** sound.

mitt

Say each picture name. Write **i** if you hear the short **i** sound.

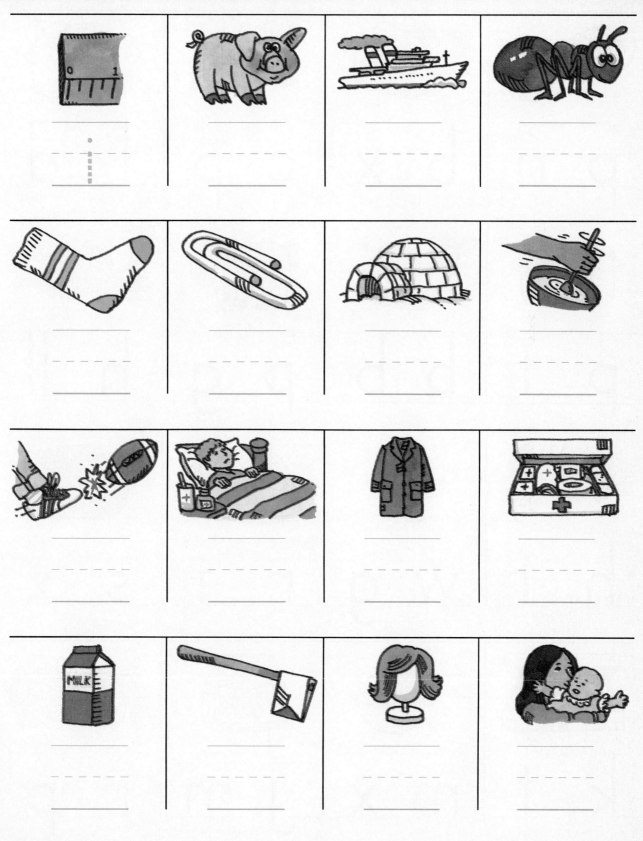

Say each picture name. Write **i** if you
hear the short **i** sound.

p n	b x	c p	l d
p t	b b	p g	h ll
h t	w g	r t	s x
k t	m x	j m	r p

Name the pictures. Color each picture
whose name rhymes with the word at
the beginning of the row.

sit			
big			
will			
nip			
win			

Name _____

Look at the letter in the box.
Draw a line from the letter to
the picture whose name
begins with the letter.

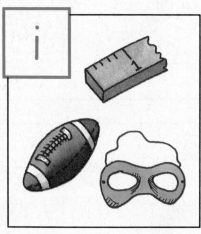

Listen to the **first** sound in each picture name. Find that letter on a crayon. Use your crayons to make each bird the right color.

Name _____

Circle the letter for the **vowel** sound.
Then write the letter.

d**a**m   f**o**x   m**i**tt

a o (i)	a o i	a o i	a o i
i			

a o i	a o i	a o i	a o i

a o i	a o i	a o i	a o i

Name the picture. Circle the word.
Write the word.

 dog
(jog)
bog

j̈ȯg̈

 hiss
miss
kiss

 nap
map
tap

 pin
tin
win

 pink
ink
mink

 sing
ring
king

 dig
pig
wig

 set
get
net

 jam
ham
dam

Name _____

Look at the picture. Then read the sentence. Circle the word that completes the sentence. Write the word on the line.

1. Jan and I _____ .

jog
bog
dog

2. We do _____ jog fast.

tot
pot
not

3. Jan has a _____ .

wig
dig
jig

4. Is the wig too _____ ?

dig
wig
big

5. Jan gave me a _____ .

win
pin
fin

6. It looks like a _____ .

bid
kid
did

Read the story. Then read the
question. Write the answer in
a complete sentence. Color the picture.

Tim

Sis pats her pig, Tim.
Tim is a big pig.
Tim is a fast pig.
Tim will win.

Who is Tim?

_____

_____

Name _____

UNIT 2: Story—Apply Short Vowel i To Decode Words in Context

Read more of the story. Then read
the question. Underline the answer
and then write it. Color the picture.

Tim got a kiss.
Tim is off.
Tim will win for his pal.
Tim will win for Sis.

Will Tim win?

Tim will win.

Tim will not win.

_____

- -

_____

Mix a Pancake

Mix a pancake,
Stir a pancake,
Pop it in the pan;
Fry the pancake,
Toss the pancake—
Catch it if you can.

Christina Rossetti

Use the name of a food to complete the poem.
Then draw a picture.

_____

Mix a _____

_____

Stir a _____
Pop it in the pan;

_____

Fry the _____

_____

Toss the _____
Catch it if you can.

Say the picture name. Write the letter that stands for the **first** sound.

_____ _____ _____

_____ _____ _____

_____ _____ _____

_____ _____ _____

_____ _____ _____

Say the picture name. Fill in the
circle next to the letter for
the **last** sound.

○ k ○ p ○ n	○ n ○ k ○ p	○ p ○ n ○ k
○ p ○ k ○ n	○ k ○ p ○ n	○ n ○ p ○ k
○ n ○ k ○ p	○ p ○ n ○ k	○ k ○ n ○ p
○ p ○ n ○ k	○ n ○ p ○ k	○ k ○ p ○ n
○ n ○ p ○ k	○ p ○ k ○ n	○ p ○ k ○ n

Cat begins with the **c** sound.
Name each picture and listen to the first sound. Color the ones that begin with the **c** sound.

C

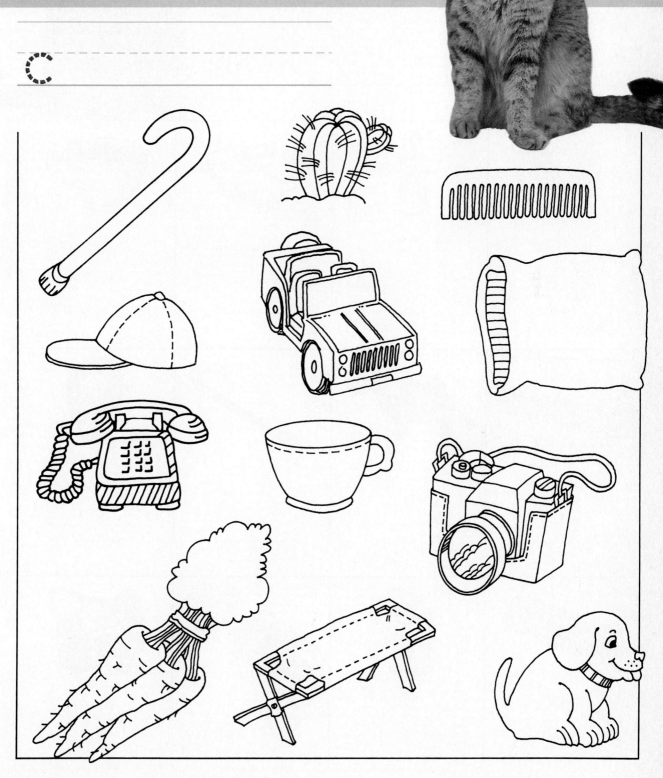

Name _____

Write c if the picture name begins with the c sound.

c

c			

Hat begins with the **h** sound.
Name each picture and listen to the first sound. Color the ones that begin with the **h** sound.

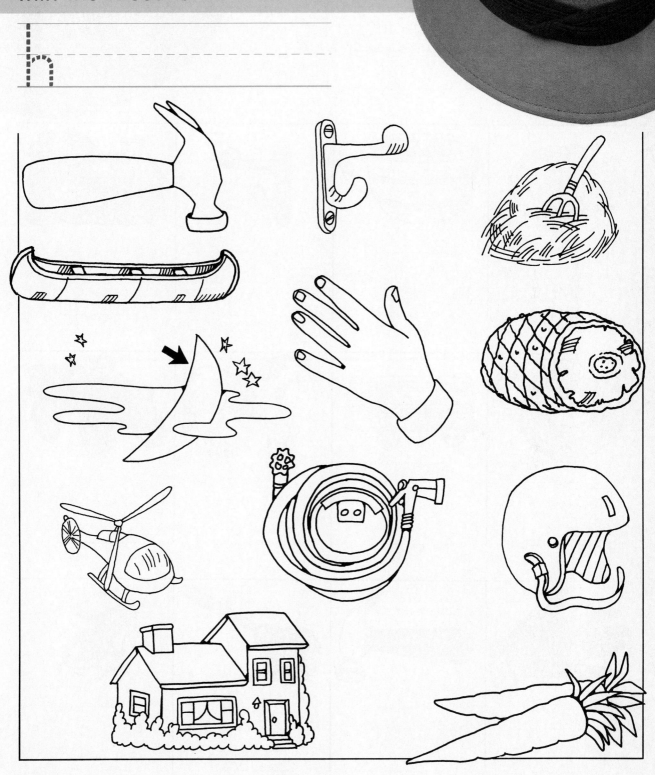

Name _____

Write **h** if the picture name begins with the **h** sound.

h

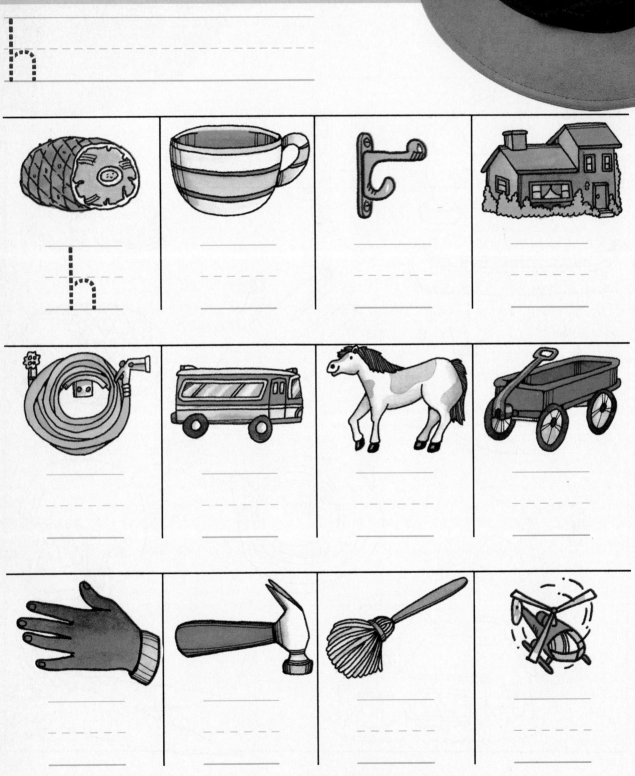

h

Leaf begins with the **l** sound.
Name each picture and listen to the first
sound. Color the ones that begin with
the **l** sound.

Name _____

Write l if the picture name begins with the l sound.

l

l			

Rake begins with the **r** sound.
Name each picture and listen to the first
sound. Color the ones that begin with
the **r** sound.

r

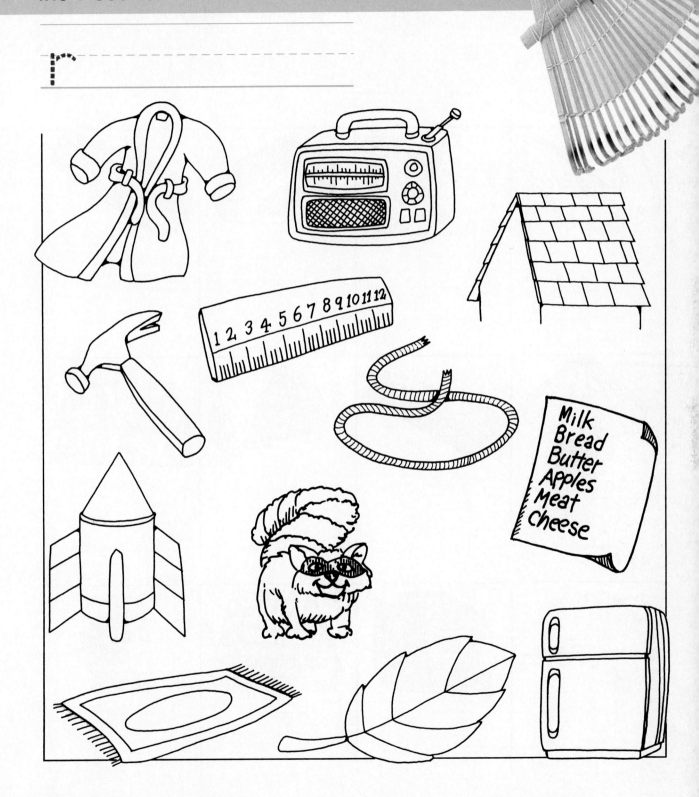

Name _____

Write **r** if the picture name begins with the **r** sound.

Umbrella begins with the short **u** sound. Name the pictures. Color those whose names begin with the short **u** sound.

Name _____

Cup has the short **u** sound.
Name the pictures. Color each picture
whose name has the short **u** sound.

cup

Say each picture name. Write **u** if you hear the short **u** sound.

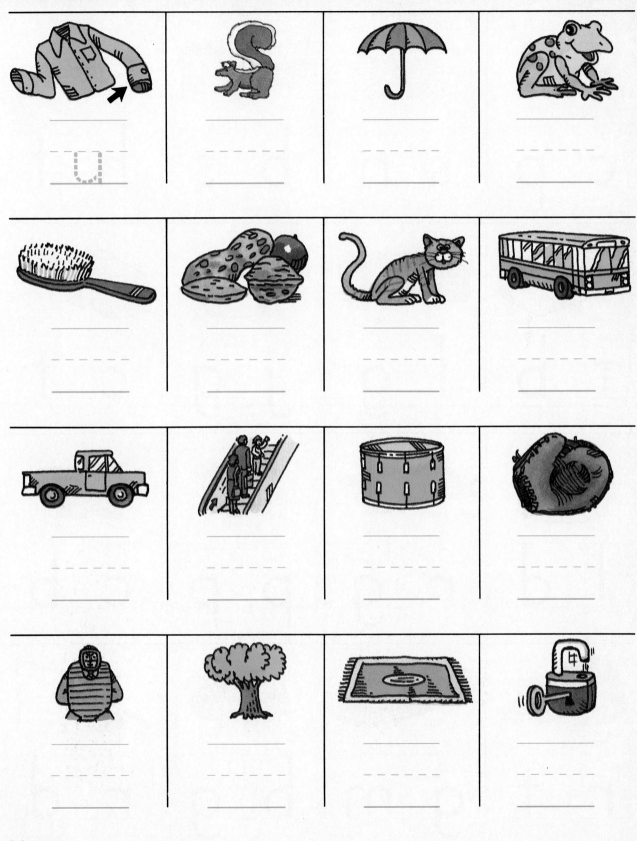

Say each picture name. Write **u** if you
hear the short **u** sound.

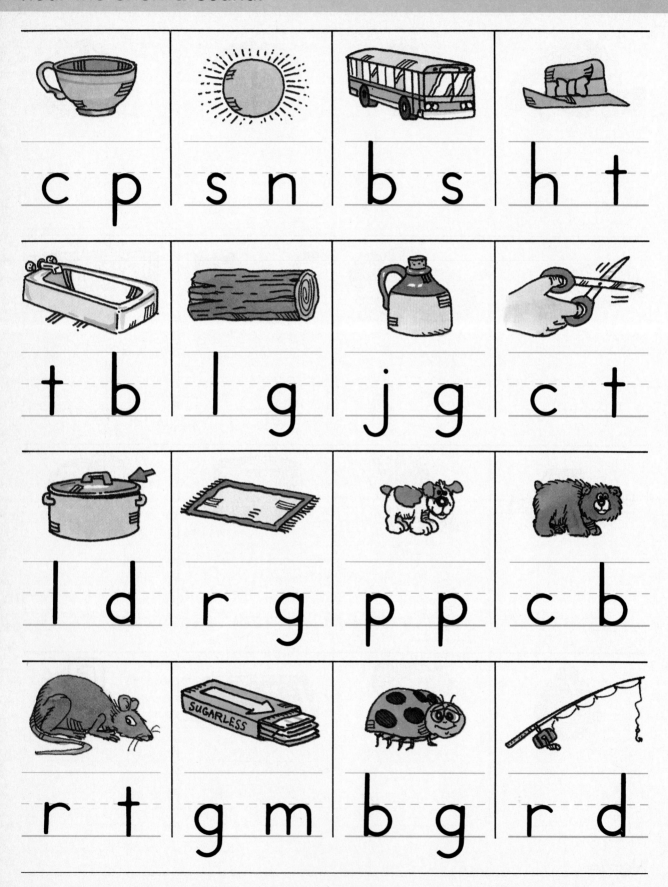

c p   s n   b s   h t

t b   l g   j g   c t

l d   r g   p p   c b

r t   g m   b g   r d

Name the pictures. Color each picture
whose name rhymes with the word at
the beginning of the row.

sum			
hug			
hut			
cub			
fun			

Name _____

UNIT 2: Short Vowel u

Look at the letter in the box.
Draw a line from the letter to
the picture whose name
begins with the letter.

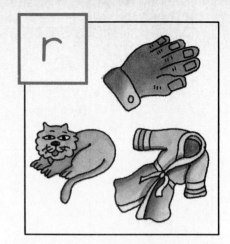

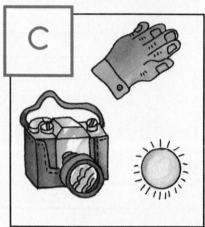

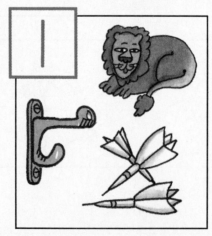

Listen to the **first** sound in each picture name. Find that letter on a crayon. Use your crayons to make each ball the right color.

Name _____

UNIT 2: Review Initial c, h, l, r, u   117

Circle the letter for the **vowel** sound.
Then write the letter.

d(a)m   f(o)x   c(u)p   m(i)tt

(a) o u	a i o	o a u	i o u
a			

i o u	a o u	i o u	a o u

a o u	a o i	a o u	i o u

Name the picture. Circle the picture name. Write the name.

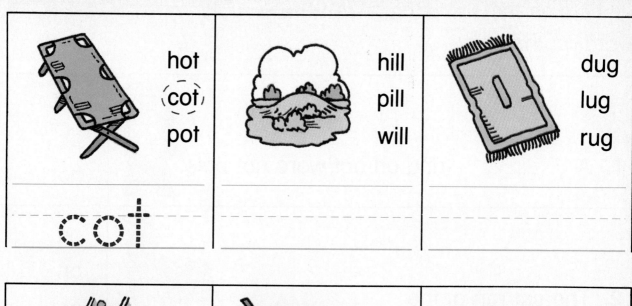

hot
(cot)
pot

cot

hill
pill
will

dug
lug
rug

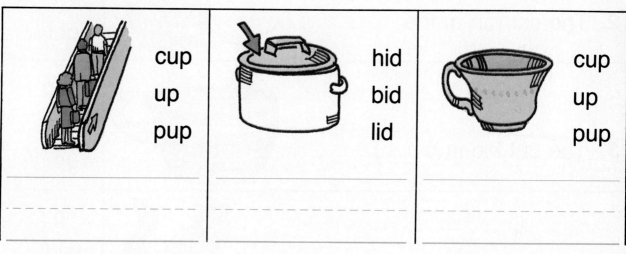

cup
up
pup

hid
bid
lid

cup
up
pup

bat
cat
hat

rat
mat
pat

fan
ran
can

Name _____

Look at the picture. Then read the sentence. Circle the word that completes the sentence. Write the word on the line.

1. A _____ and an ant were not pals.

cat
at
hat

2. The cat ran at the _____ .

an
on
ant

3. The ant hid in a _____ .

cap
cup
up

4. The cat sat on a _____ .

rig
rag
rug

5. Can the ant _____ up?

hot
hop
hat

6. Will it _____ on the cat?

and
land
hand

Read the story. Read the sentences in
the box. Write the sentences that come
first, next, and last. Color the picture.

Gus Has Fun

The sun is up.
Gus is up.
Gus is a duck.
Gus runs in the mud.
The mud is fun.

Gus runs.
The sun is up.
Gus is up.

First: _____

Next: _____

Last: _____

Name _____

Read more of the story. Then read the
question. Underline the answer and then
write the answer. Color the picture.

Russ rubs Gus in the tub.
Gus has fun in the suds.
But Gus must nap on the rug.

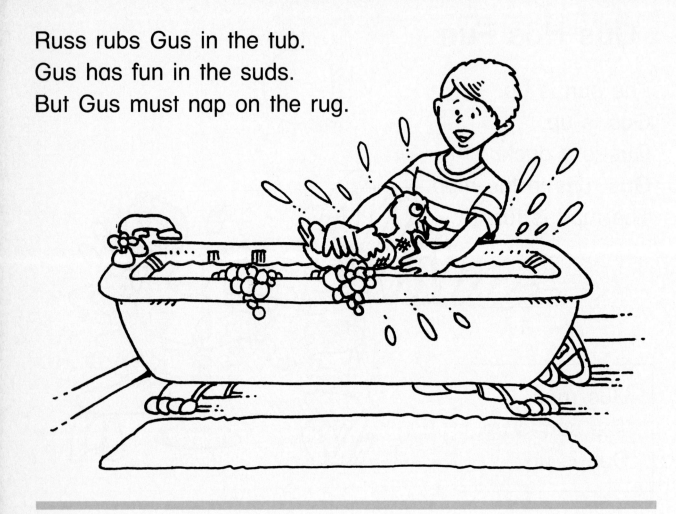

Why is Gus in a tub?

Gus is a duck.

Gus ran in mud.

Gus must nap.

The Way They Scrub

The way they scrub
Me in the tub,
I think there's
    Hardly
    Any
    Doubt
Sometime they'll rub
And rub and rub
Until they simply
    Rub
    Me
    Out.

A. B. Ross

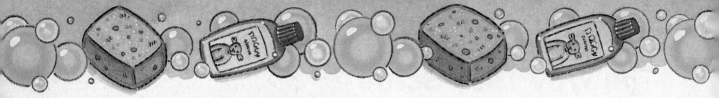

What is the best way to give a dog a bath?
Draw a picture.
Show what you would do.

Write three steps for giving a dog a bath.

How to Give a Dog a Bath

Step 1 _____

Step 2 _____

Step 3 _____

Say the picture name. Write the letter that stands for the **first** sound.

UNIT 2: Assess c, h, l, r, u   125

Say the picture name. Fill in the
circle next to the letter for
the **vowel** sound.

○ u ○ a ○ i	○ i ○ u ○ a	○ a ○ i ○ o
○ i ○ u ○ o	○ u ○ a ○ i	○ o ○ u ○ i
○ o ○ u ○ a	○ a ○ i ○ u	○ a ○ o ○ u
○ a ○ i ○ u	○ u ○ i ○ o	○ i ○ u ○ a
○ u ○ o ○ i	○ u ○ o ○ a	○ u ○ a ○ o

Vest begins with the **v** sound.
Name each picture and listen to the
first sound. Color the ones that begin
with the **v** sound.

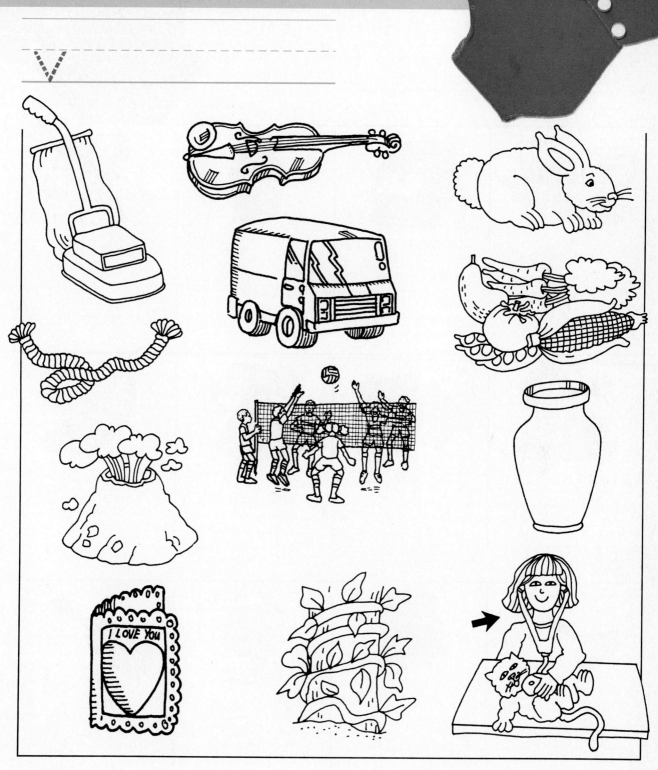

Name _____

Write **v** if the picture name begins with the **v** sound.

V

			(vest image)
V			

Yarn begins with the **y** sound.
Name each picture and listen to the first
sound. Color the ones that begin with
the **y** sound.

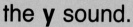

Name _____

Write **y** if the picture name begins with the **y** sound.

y

y			

Zipper begins with the **z** sound.
Name each picture and listen to the first
sound. Color the ones that begin with
the **z** sound.

Z

Name _____

Write **z** if the picture name begins with the **z** sound.

Quilt begins with the **qu** sound.

Name each picture and listen to the first sound.

Color the ones that begin with the **qu** sound.

Write **qu** if the name begins with the first sound in **quilt.**

Name _____

Name each picture below. Listen to the **last** sound. Color the pictures that end with the **x** sound in **ax.**

Write **x** if the name ends with the **last** sound in **ax.**

Circle the letter for the **last** sound.
Then write the letter.

 nail five  ox

l Ⓘ v x	l v x	l v x	l v x
l			

l v x	l v x	l v x	l v x

l v x	l v x	l v x	l v x

Name _____

UNIT 2: Final Consonants l, v, x 135

Write the missing letter to complete each word.

lad van ox et

a sea og bo

gir fo est wa

mi eg si hee

Egg begins with the short **e** sound.
Name the pictures. Color those whose
names begin with the short **e** sound.

Name _____

Jet has the short **e** sound. Name
the pictures. Color each picture whose
name has the short **e** sound.

jet

Say each picture name. Write **e** if you hear the short **e** sound.

Say each picture name. Write **e** if you
hear the short **e** sound.

n t p n b s w b

z p l g b d j g

w t g s m n v t

t n j t v n l g

Name the pictures. Color each picture whose name rhymes with the word at the beginning of the row.

vet

den

fell

fed

peg

Name _____

Look at the letter in the box. Draw a line from the letter to the picture whose name **begins** with the letter.

v

qu

e

y

qu

z

e

v

y

z

Listen to the **first** sound in each picture name. Find that letter on a crayon. Use your crayons to make each bone the right color.

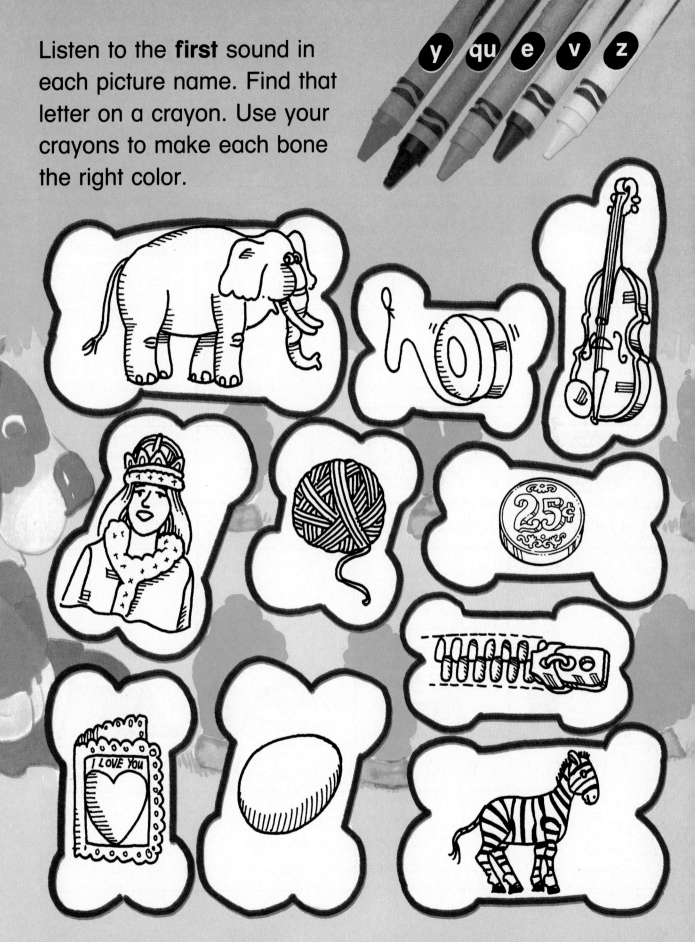

Name _____

UNIT 2: Review Initial v, y, z, qu, e   143

Circle the letter for the **vowel** sound.
Then write the letter.

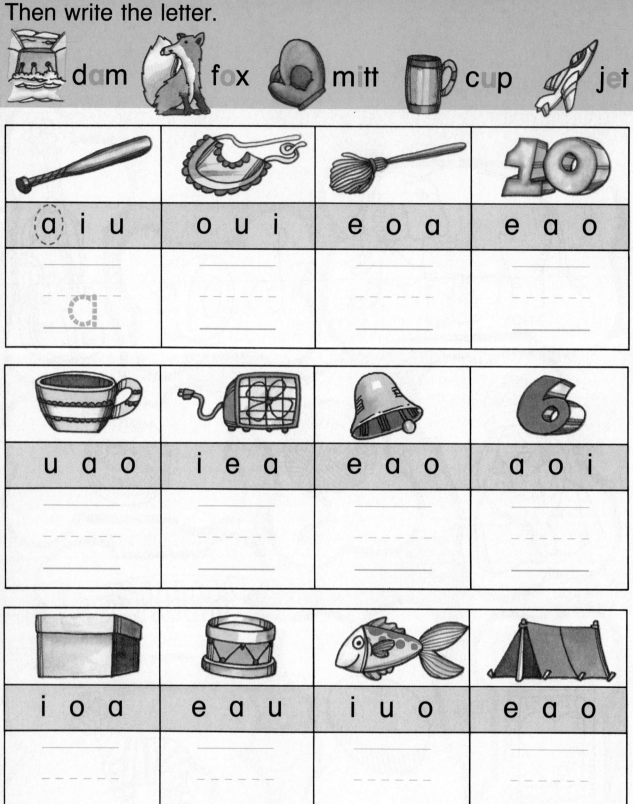

dam   fox   mitt   cup   jet

(a) i u	o u i	e o a	e a o
a			
u a o	i e a	e a o	a o i
i o a	e a u	i u o	e a o

Name the picture. Circle the picture name. Write the name.

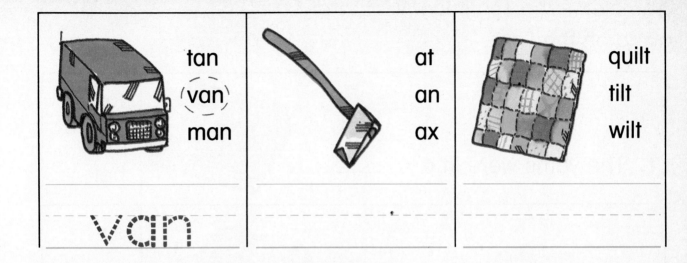

tan	at	quilt
(van)	an	tilt
man	ax	wilt

van

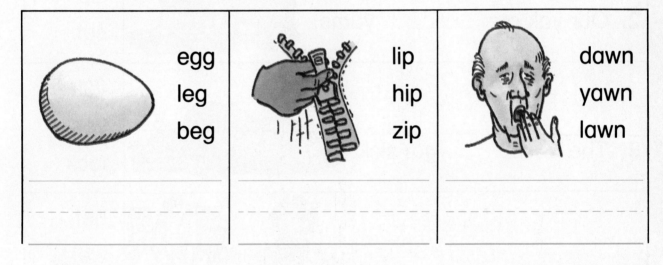

egg	lip	dawn
leg	hip	yawn
beg	zip	lawn

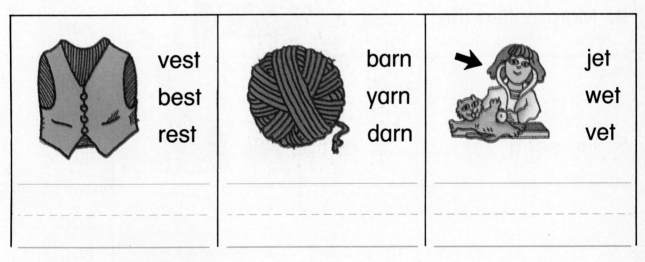

vest	barn	jet
best	yarn	wet
rest	darn	vet

Name _____

Look at the picture. Then read the sentence. Circle the word that completes the sentence. Write the word on the line.

I. The yams were in a _____ .		fox box bet
2. Our yak ate _____ yams.		six sip set
3. The _____ got sick.		yak yes tack
4. Mom called the _____ .		bet wet vet
5. He set a _____ on the yak.		quilt built tilt
6. The vet left for the _____ .		zap zoo zest

Say the picture name. Circle the letter
for the **middle** sound. Then write
the letter.

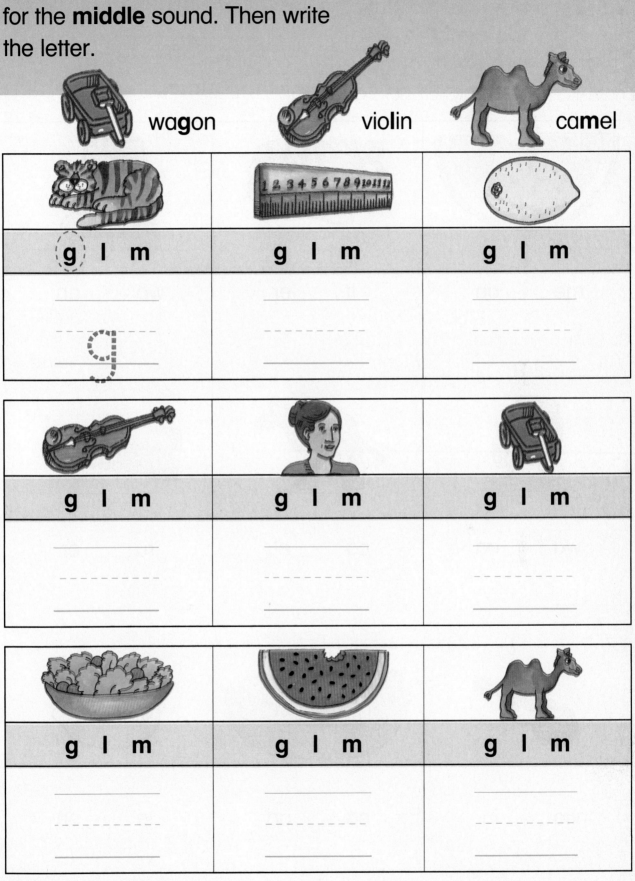

wa**g**on   vio**l**in   ca**m**el

g l m   g l m   g l m

g

g l m   g l m   g l m

g l m   g l m   g l m

Name _____

UNIT 2: Medial Consonants g, l, m

Say the picture name. Write the letter that stands for the **middle** sound.

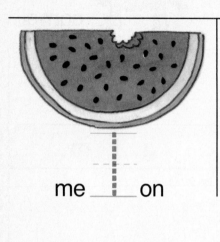 me __ on

 ti __ er

 wo __ an

 wa __ on

 ca __ el

 ru __ er

vio __ in

 sa __ ad

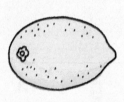 le __ on

Name _____

148   UNIT 2: Medial Consonants g, l, m

Say the picture name. Circle the letter
for the **middle** sound. Then write
the letter.

money   seven   guitar

n (t) v	n t v	n t v
t		

n t v	n t v	n t v

n t v	n t v	n t v

Name _____

UNIT 2: **Medial Consonants n, t, v**   149

Say the picture name. Write the letter that
stands for the **middle** sound.

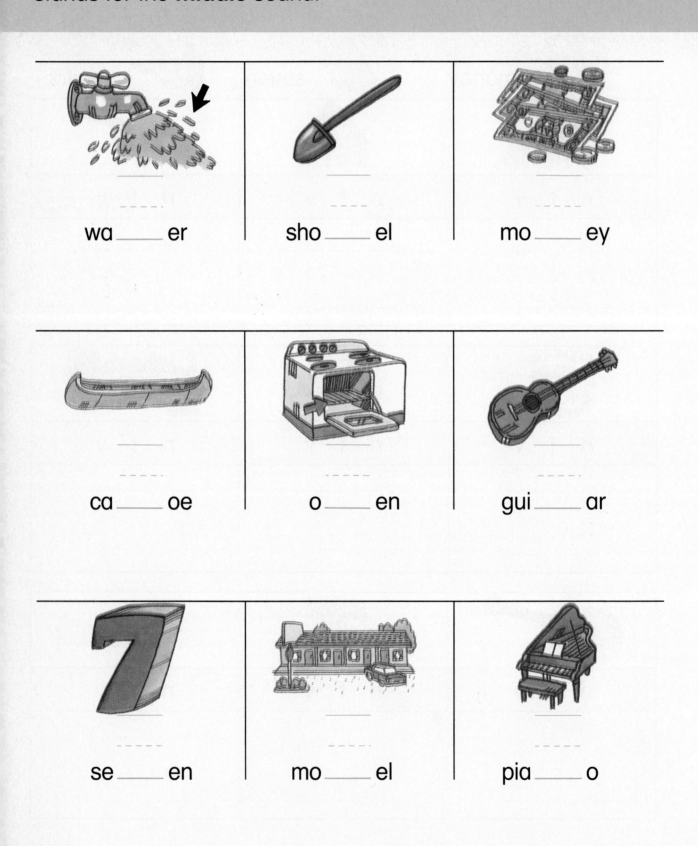

wa ___ er

sho ___ el

mo ___ ey

ca ___ oe

o ___ en

gui ___ ar

se ___ en

mo ___ el

pia ___ o

Name _____

Read the story. Then read the
questions. Write the answers in
complete sentences. Color the picture.

Nell the Hen

Ken has a pet hen.
Nell is a red hen.
Nell is in the pen.
Nell has a bad leg.
Nell fell on her leg.

Who is Nell?

_____

_____

Where is Nell?

_____

_____

Name _____

Read more of the story. Then read the questions. Write the answers in complete sentences. Color the picture.

Ken is at the vet with Nell.
The vet can tell that Nell fell.
The vet will set the leg.
Yes, Nell will get well.

Who will help Nell?
_____

_____

How will the vet help?
_____

_____

Will Nell get well?
_____

_____

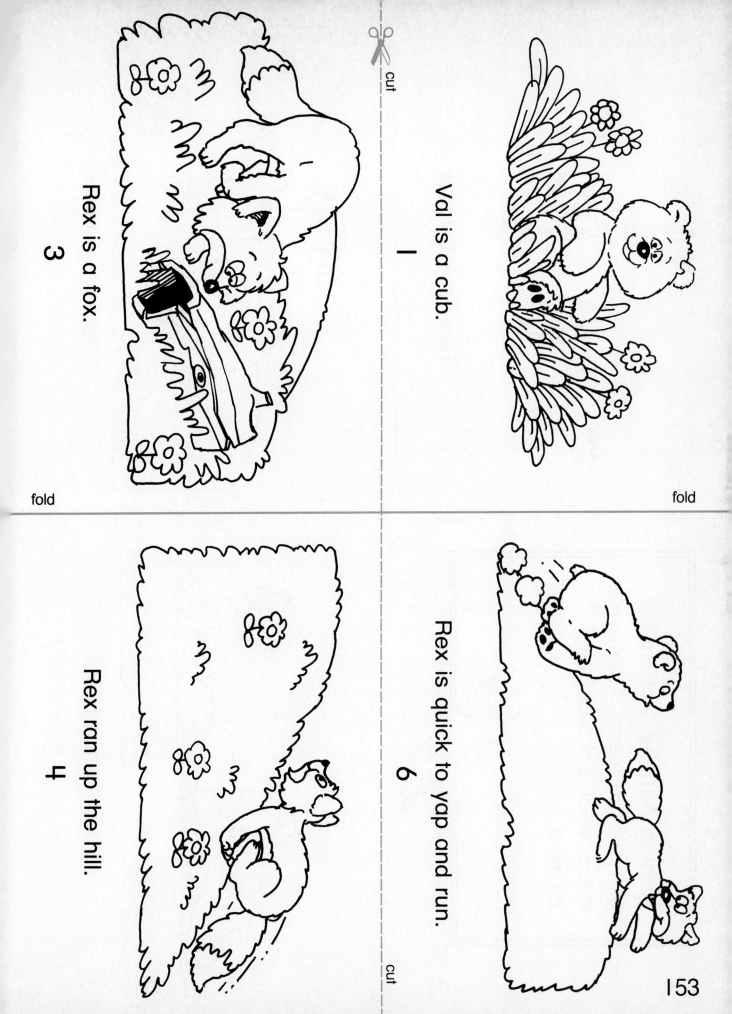

cut

Val is a cub.

1

fold

Rex is a fox.

3

fold

Rex is quick to yap and run.

6

cut

153

Rex ran up the hill.

4

Val

This book belongs to

_____

Val ran up the hill.

2

Writing Activity: Act out the story with a friend. Then write about what Val and Rex do next.

154

Val ran to hug him.

5

Say the picture name. Write the letter that stands for the **first** sound.

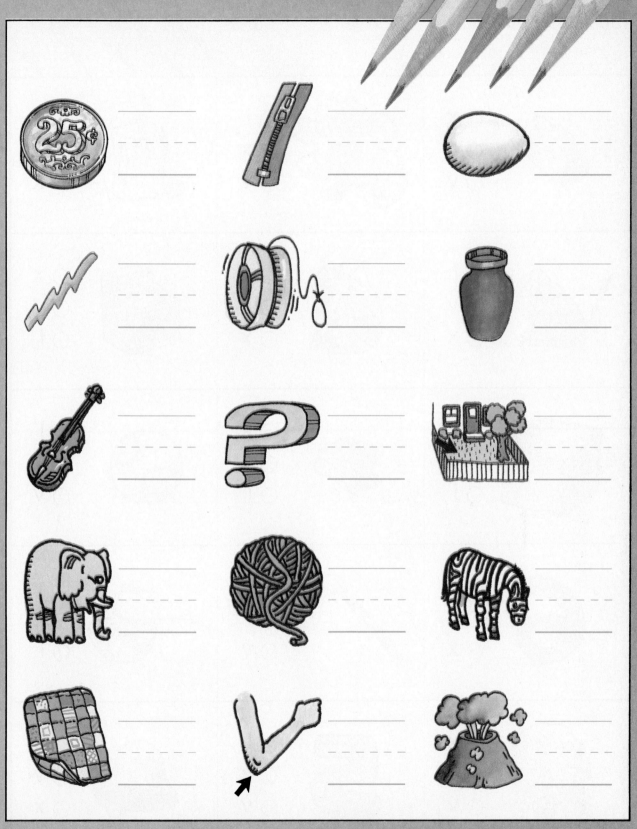

Say the picture name. Fill in the
circle next to the letter for
the **last** sound.

○ x ○ l ○ v	○ l ○ x ○ v	○ v ○ l ○ x
○ l ○ v ○ x	○ v ○ l ○ x	○ x ○ v ○ l
○ v ○ x ○ l	○ x ○ v ○ l	○ l ○ x ○ v
○ l ○ v ○ x	○ x ○ l ○ v	○ v ○ x ○ l
○ x ○ l ○ v	○ l ○ x ○ v	○ l ○ v ○ x

The long **a** sound is heard in **rake**.
Name each picture. Color the picture if
you hear the long **a** sound.

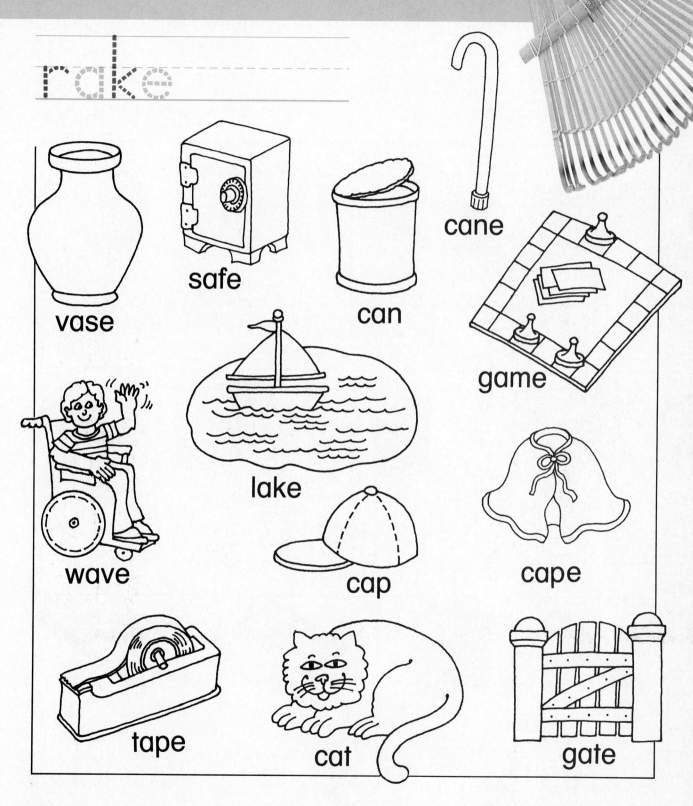

rake

vase

safe

can

cane

game

wave

lake

cap

cape

tape

cat

gate

Name _____

Name each picture. Write the name
with **a-e** if you hear the long **a**
sound in **rake**.

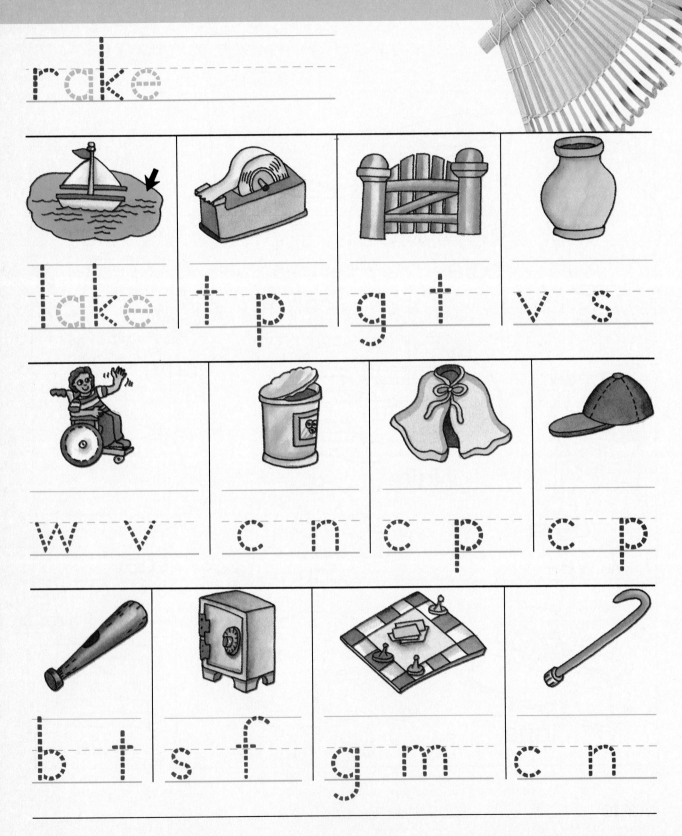

rake

lake   t p   g t   v s

w v   c n   c p   c p

b t   s f   g m   c n

Name each picture. Circle the picture name.
Write the name.

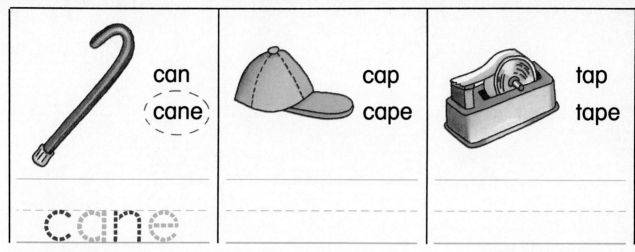

can
(cane)

cane

cap
cape

tap
tape

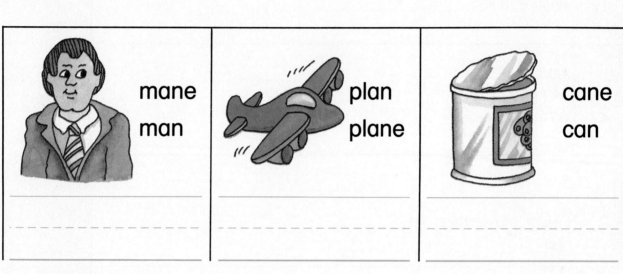

mane
man

plan
plane

cane
can

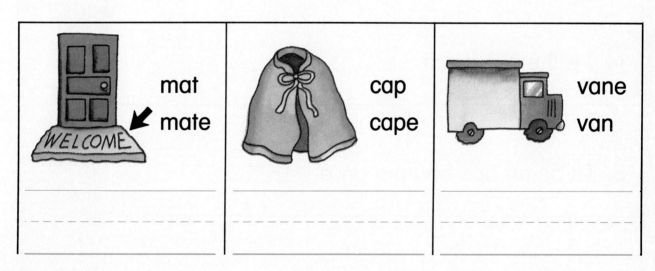

mat
mate

cap
cape

vane
van

Name _____

Read each sentence. Circle the word that completes the sentence. Write the word on the line.

1. Name this _____ .		game got get
2. I will _____ a mask .		mad make met
3. It will look like an _____ .		am an ape
4. I will make it with _____ .		tap tape tan
5. I'll be an ape and put on a _____ .		cape cave cat
6. I am a good _____ !		fat fad fake

The letters **ai** and **ay** can stand for the
long a sound. Name each picture.
Circle the picture name. Write the
name. Color the picture.

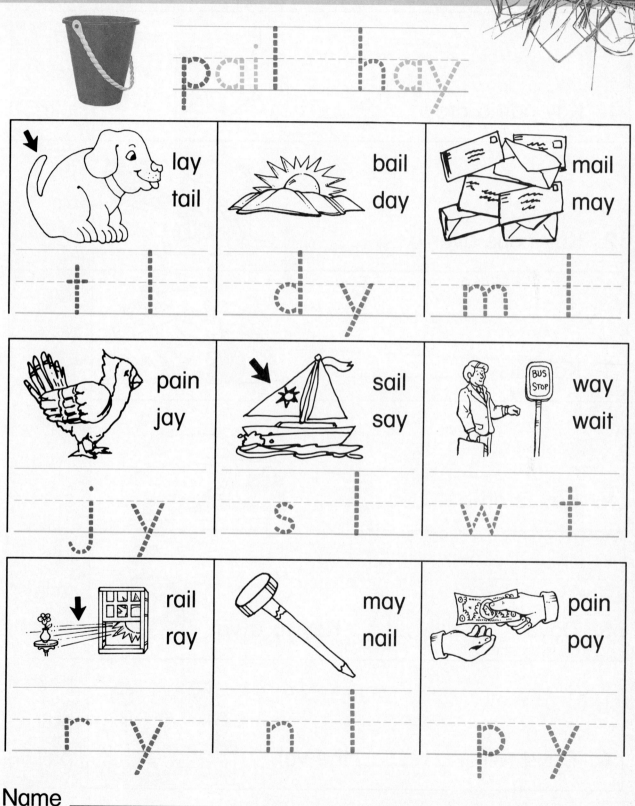

pail   hay

lay
tail

t l

bail
day

d y

mail
may

m l

pain
jay

j y

sail
say

s l

way
wait

w t

rail
ray

r y

may
nail

n l

pain
pay

p y

Name _____

Read each sentence. Circle the word that completes the sentence. Write the word on the line.

1. Kay has a gray _____ .	hay tail take
2. Kay hops over a _____ .	rake ray rain
3. Kay hits a _____ .	lap pay pail
4. Kay is on a _____ .	nail name may
5. Dave _____ Kay to a vet.	lays tails takes
6. Dave will _____ the vet.	bake pay pail

Read the story. Choose the best title.
Circle it. Then write it on the top line.
Color the picture.

_____

- -

_____

James and Kay went to fish at the lake.
James will wade in the lake.
Kay got the pail of bait.
Kay gave James the bait.
It made a fun day.

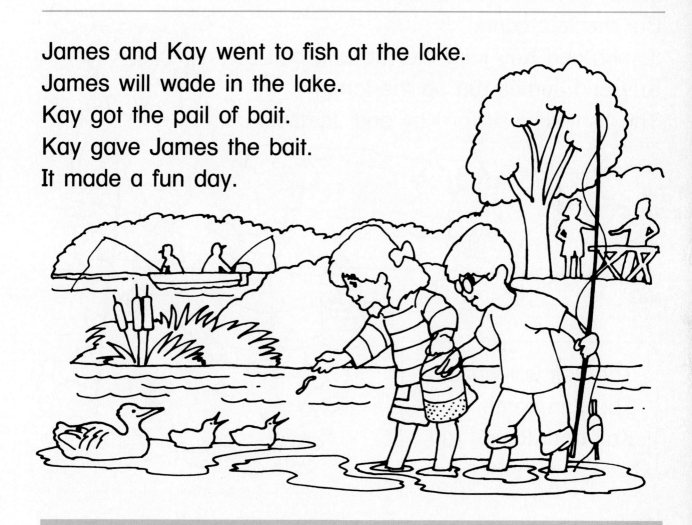

The Pail of Bait

A Day at the Lake

Fish Can Wade

Name _____

UNIT 3: Story—Apply Long Vowel a To Decode Words in Context

Read more of the story. Read the sentences in the box. Write the sentences that come first, next, and last. Color the picture.

A fish gave the rod a tug.
But the rain came.
James and Kay take the rod and bait.
Kay and James run up the lane.
The fish will wait for Kay and James.

The fish will wait.
The rain came.
Kay and James ran.

First: _____

_____

Next: _____

_____

Last: _____

The long **i** sound is heard in **kite.** Name each picture. Color the picture if you hear the long **i** sound.

kite

six

mice

dive

vine

bib

five

pig

ice

nine

pine

bike

dime

Name _____

Name each picture. Write the name
with **i-e** if you hear the long **i**
sound in **kite**.

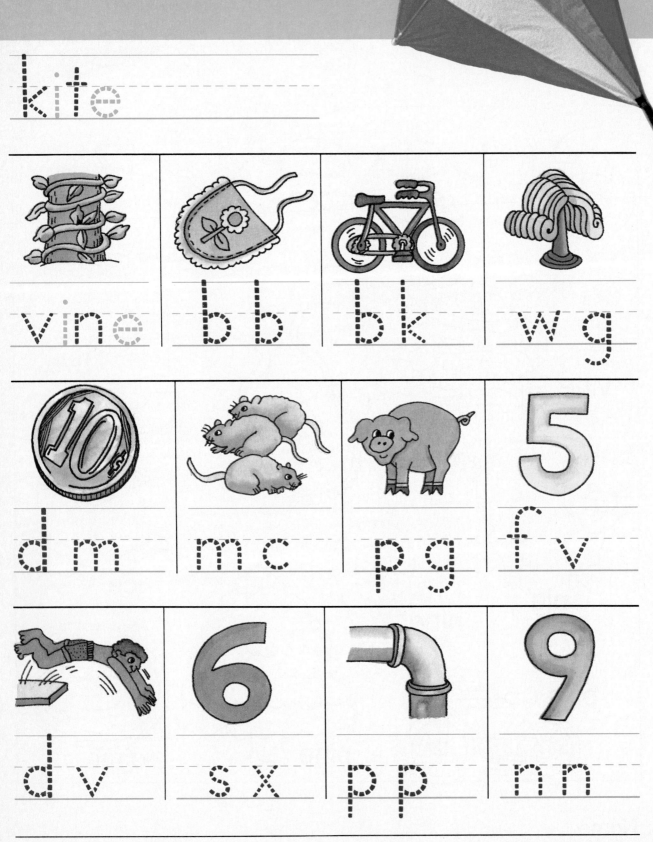

k i t e

v i n e   b   b   b   k   w   g

d   m   m   c   p   g   f   v

d   v   s   x   p   p   n   n

Read the words and look at the
pictures. Draw a line from each word
to the picture it names. Color the pictures.

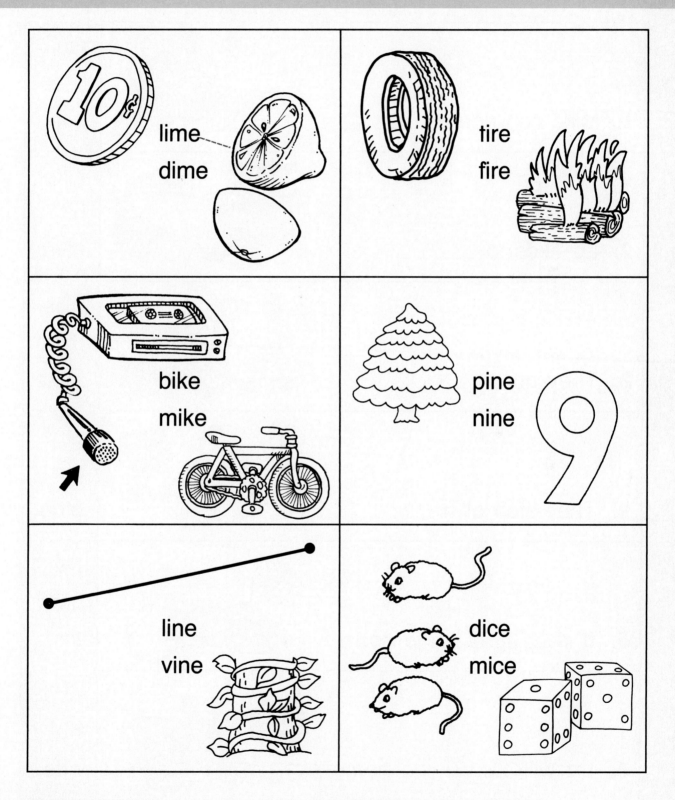

lime
dime

tire
fire

bike
mike

pine
nine

line
vine

dice
mice

Name _____

UNIT 3: Apply Long Vowel i To Decode Words 167

Read each sentence. Circle the word
that completes the sentence. Write
the word on the line.

1. Mike can ride a _____ .		big bike bite
2. Liz likes to _____ .		hike hit hive
3. They go a _____ .		mile mill mine
4. They stop at a _____ .		pipe pin pine
5. It is _____ to go.		tile time tin
6. Liz will _____ home.		ripe rib ride

Name each picture. Circle the picture name.
Write the name.

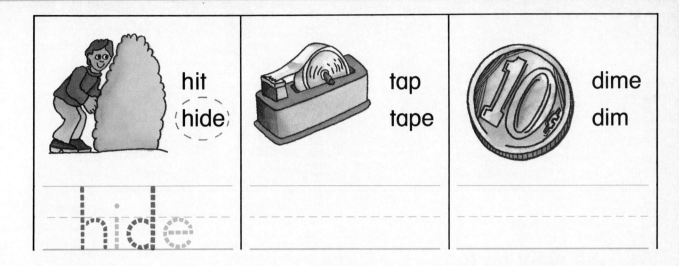

hit
(hide)

tap
tape

dime
dim

hide

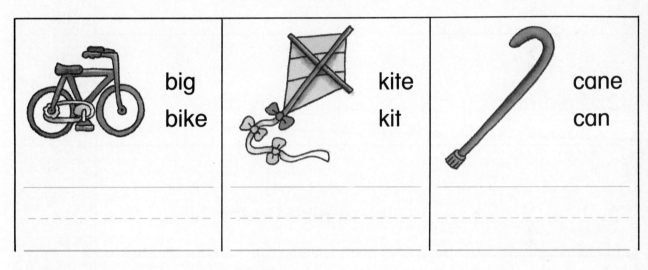

big
bike

kite
kit

cane
can

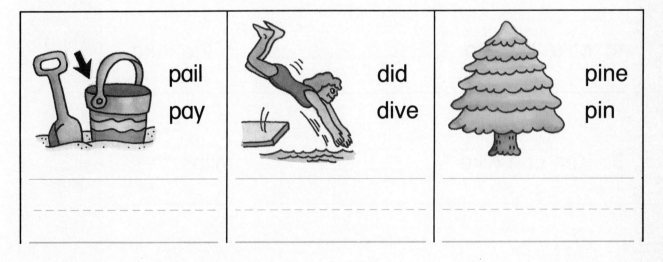

pail
pay

did
dive

pine
pin

Name _____

Read each sentence. Circle the word that completes the sentence. Write the word on the line.

1. We went on a _____.	hike hide him
2. I did not _____ my bike.	rid ripe ride
3. I _____ to hike up the hill.	live like lip
4. Mike likes to _____ in the lake.	dime dive dad
5. Kim can hike _____ miles.	hive file five
6. We had a good _____.	tin tame time

Read the story. Then read the
question. Underline the answer.
Then write it. Color the picture.

The Mice

Nine mice run on a pile of logs.
The logs are pine.
The mice run on the five logs.
It is a fun time.
But a cat is in the vines.

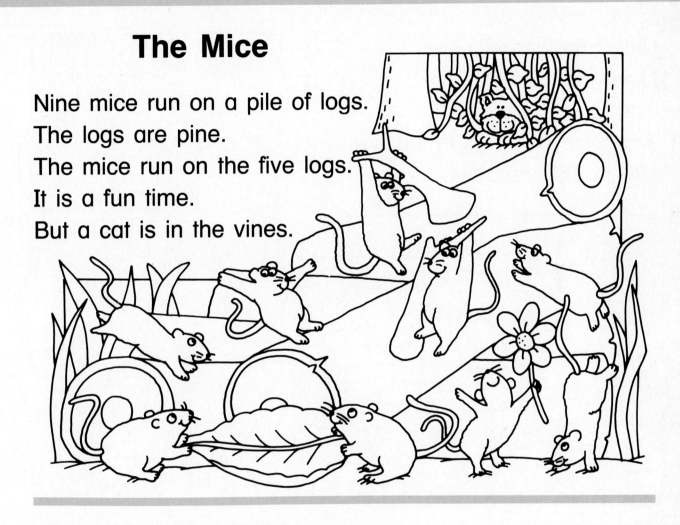

What can a cat do with mice?

It can pet mice.

It can bite mice.

It can ride mice.

Name _____

Read more of the story. Then read the
question. Underline the answer.
Then write it. Color the picture.

Nine mice make a line.
Nine mice run to a tire.
The tire is wide.
The mice can hide in the tire.
Life in the tire is fine.

Why is life in the tire fine?

Mice bite the tire.

Vines lay in the tire.

Mice hide in the tire.

_____

_____

_____

The long **o** sound is heard in **bone**.
Name each picture. Color the picture if
you hear the long **o** sound.

b o n e

robe

fox

rope

pot

home

mop

note

rose

hose

log

top

cone

Name _____

Name each picture. Write the name
with **o-e** if you hear the long **o**
sound in **bone**.

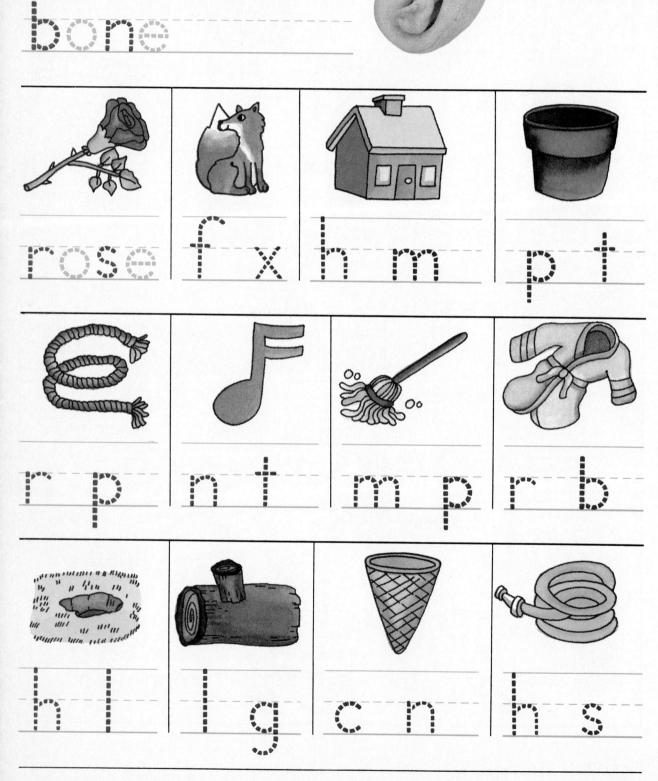

bone

rose   f   x   h   m   p   t

r   p   n   t   m   p   r   b

h   l   l   g   c   n   h   s

Name each picture. Circle the picture name.
Write the name.

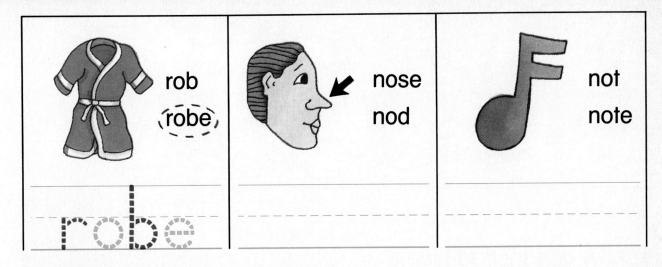

rob
(robe)

r o b e

nose
nod

not
note

dime
dim

man
mane

rope
rob

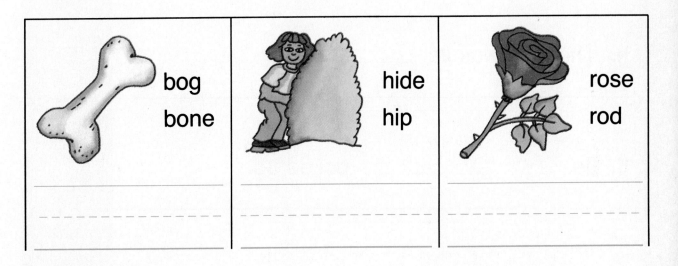

bog
bone

hide
hip

rose
rod

Name _____

Read each sentence. Circle the word that completes the sentence. Write the word on the line.

1. A dog tried to hide a _____ .		bone bop bite
2. He dug a big _____ .		hot hole hope
3. He _____ up a mole.		wave wit woke
4. The hole was its _____ .		hope hip home
5. Its _____ poked up.		nose note nod
6. Is this a big _____?		joke jade jog

The long **o** is heard in **coat**. Name each picture. Color the picture if you hear the long **o** sound.

coat

boat

goal

top

road

foal

goat

soap

coat

cot

rod

fox

toad

Name

Name each picture. Write the name with
o-e or **oa** when you hear the long **o**
sound. Color the pictures.

coat bone

t o a d   n _ _ t   b _ _ t

g _ _ t   h _ s   c _ _ t

f _ l   c _ n   n _ s

Read the story. Choose the best
title. Circle it. Then write it on
the top line. Color the picture.

_____

- - - - - - - - - - - - - - - - - -

_____

A goat and a foal are pals.
The goat and foal go up the road.
They hope to get home at five.
On the way they met a toad.
The toad rode on the foal.

Pals on the Road

The Toad Hops Home

The Foal Rode Home

Name _____

UNIT 3: Story—Apply Long Vowel o To Decode Words in Context

Read more of the story. Read the
questions. Write the answers on the
lines. Color the picture.

The goat made a joke.
The toad let go of the foal.
The toad fell in a mud hole.
But the toad is fine.
The toad likes to soak in mud.

1. Who made a joke? _____

2. Who fell in a hole? _____

3. Who likes the mud? _____

The long **u** sound is heard in **cube**.
Name each picture. Color the picture if
you hear the long **u** sound.

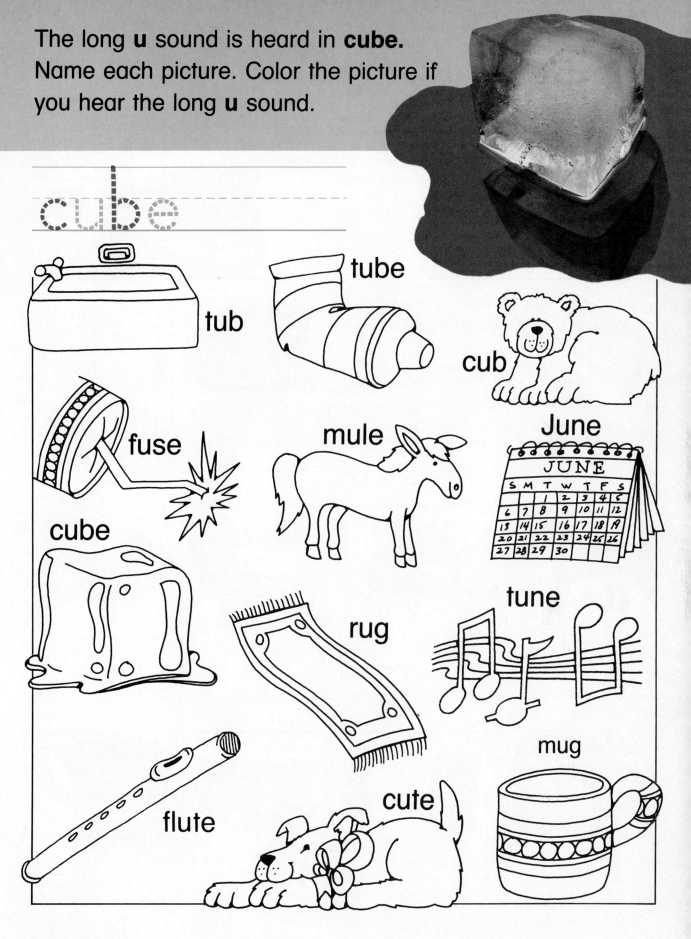

cube

tub

tube

cub

fuse

mule

June

JUNE

cube

rug

tune

flute

cute

mug

Name _____

Name each picture. Write the name
with **u-e** if you hear the long **u**
sound in **cube**.

cube

tube   c_b   c_b   t_b

m_l   b_g   t_n   c_t

j_n   f_s   b_s   m_g

Read the words and look at the
pictures. Draw a line from each word
to the picture it names. Color the pictures.

prune

tune

cube

tube

mule

Yule

fuse

use

dune

June

JUNE

flute

cute

Name

UNIT 3: Long Vowel u   183

Read each sentence. Circle the word that completes the sentence. Write the word on the line.

1. Luke is on a _____ .		tube tub rule
2. The tube is _____ .		hug cube huge
3. _____ has fun.		Bug Luke Tune
4. Then he rides a _____ .		mule rule dune
5. The mule is _____ .		cube cute hug
6. Luke hums a _____ .		tune tube dune

Name each picture. Circle the picture name. Write the name.

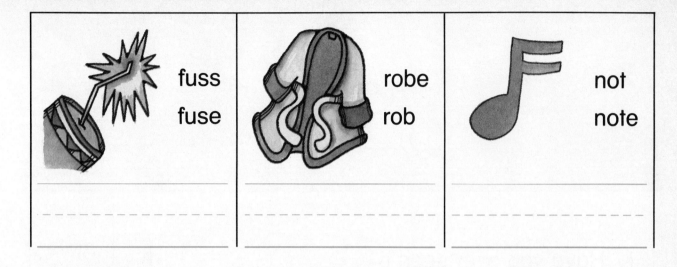

fuss
fuse

_____
- - - - - - - - - -

robe
rob

_____
- - - - - - - - - -

not
note

_____
- - - - - - - - - -

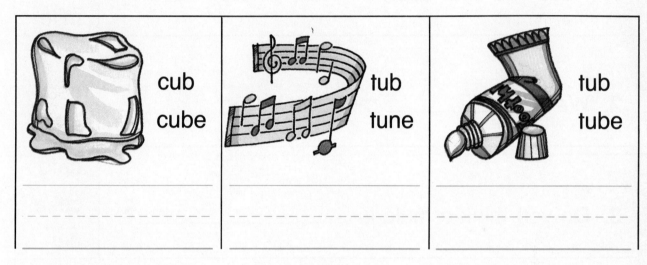

cub
cube

_____
- - - - - - - - - -

tub
tune

_____
- - - - - - - - - -

tub
tube

_____
- - - - - - - - - -

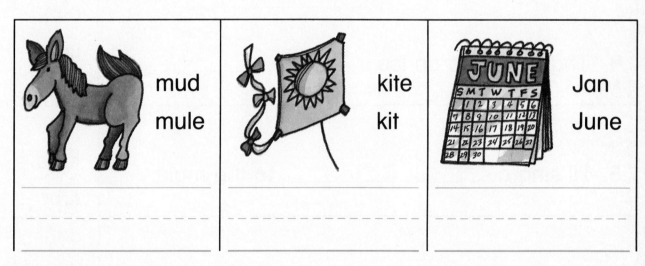

mud
mule

_____
- - - - - - - - - -

kite
kit

_____
- - - - - - - - - -

Jan
June

_____
- - - - - - - - - -

Name _____

Read each sentence. Circle the word
that completes the sentence. Write the
word on the line.

1. Have you ever seen a _____ ?	mud mule mile
2. We _____ mules to ride.	us use fuse
3. Do you think a mule is _____ ?	cute cake cut
4. That mule ate an ice _____ .	cub cute cube
5. I'll sing a _____ to the mule.	ten tune tube
6. Mules have fun in the sun in _____ .	Jan Jane June

Read the story. Read the sentences.
Write the words that complete the
sentences. Color the picture.

Duke

Duke has a flute.
The flute is in a case.
Duke got the flute.
A flute is like a tube.
The flute is not huge.

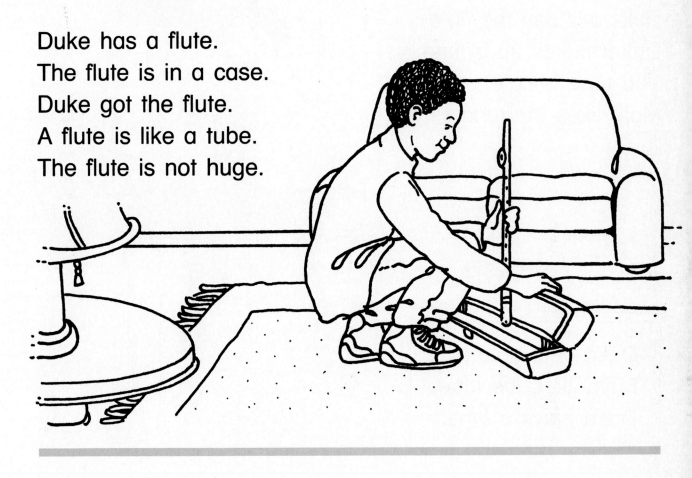

_____

1. _____ has a flute.

2. The _____ is in a case.

3. A flute is like a _____ .

Name _____

Read more of the story. Then read the sentences in the box. Write the sentences that come first, next, and last. Color the picture.

Duke will use the flute.
Duke makes up a tune.
The tune is cute.
Mom likes the tune.

Duke gets a flute.
Mom likes the tune.
Duke plays a tune.

First: _____

Next: _____

Last: _____

The long **e** sound is heard in **leaf** and **bee.** Name each picture. Color the picture if you hear the long **e** sound.

leaf bee

bed

tent

team

seal

weed

tea

queen

vest

men

jeep

peas

Name _____

Name each picture. Write the missing letters and trace the vowel letters.

l_ _ f   b_ _

   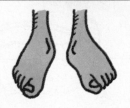

_ _ ea   _ _ ea   _ _ ea   _ _ ee

_ _ ea   _ _ ee   _ _ ea   _ _ ea

   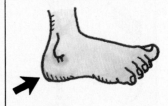

_ _ ea   _ _ ee   _ _ ea   _ _ ee

Name each picture. Circle the picture
name. Write the name. Color the
picture.

peel
pet

_____

mitt
meet

_____

peek
poke

_____

tame
team

_____

peak
pack

_____

seed
seat

_____

bean
bee

_____

lake
leak

_____

red
read

_____

Name _____

Read each sentence. Circle the word that completes the sentence. Write the word on the line.

1. It is time to _____ .	feet meal eat
2. I like to eat _____ .	meat mean need
3. I like to eat _____ .	pails peeks peas
4. I like baked _____ .	deeds beaks beans
5. I _____ full.	fell feel feet
6. The _____ was fine.	meal mean read

Name each picture. Circle the picture name. Write the name.

sell
seal

beak
bake

cub
cube

tube
tub

fit
feet

meat
met

wed
weed

bee
bet

pine
pin

Name _____

UNIT 3: Review Long Vowels e, u, i **193**

Read each sentence. Circle the word that completes the sentence. Write the word on the line.

1. A cat asked a dog to _____.	_____	tea take time
2. "I like tea," said the dog, _____.	_____	Lee Cat Bee
3. "Then," said Cat, "we'll go to _____."	_____	set sit sea
4. "We'll take as a pet a bumble _____."	_____	bee bet bit
5. "Not I," said Bee. "Take the big _____."	_____	seal feel mad
6. "Fine," said Cat, "we made a _____."	_____	deal seat deep

Read the story. Then read the sentences.
Write the words that complete the
sentences. Color the picture.

The Sea

The seal leaps to the sea.
The seal will go to the deep sea.
Fish are in the deep sea.
The seal likes to eat fish.
The seal will eat a big meal.

_____

1. The _____ leaps.

2. It will go to the deep _____ .

3. The seal likes to _____ fish.

Name _____

Read more of the story. Then read the
sentences in the box. Write the sentences
that come first, next, and last.
Color the picture.

A fish eats by the weed.
The seal does not see the fish.
But the fish sees the seal.
The fish hides in the weed.

The fish sees a seal.
The fish eats.
The fish hides.

First: ------------------------------------

Next: ------------------------------------

Last: ------------------------------------

Say each picture name. Circle the word that names each picture. If you hear the **y** sound in **baby,** color the picture red. If you hear the **y** sound in **fly,** color the picture blue. Then circle the word.

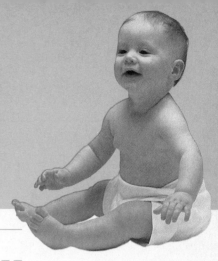

fly baby

puppy
pig

fit
fry

pet
penny

lady
lad

cat
cry

funny
fan

dry
drum

pony
pot

cry
candy

sky
skate

try
twenty

bus
bunny

Name _____

Say each picture name.
Write the picture name.

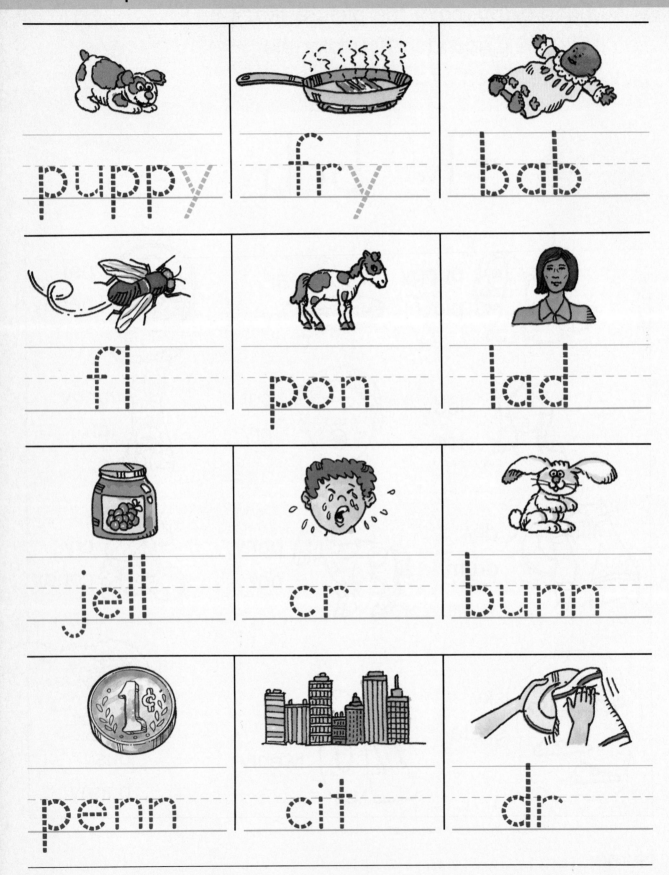

puppy

fry

bab

fl

pon

lad

jell

cr

bunn

penn

cit

dr

Listen to the **vowel** sound in each picture name. Find that vowel on a crayon. Use your crayons to make each flag the right color.

Name _____

Name each picture. Write the vowels to complete the words.

g m ___ ___   r ___ p ___   t ___ ___ l   f ___ v ___

b ___ k ___   m ___ l ___   j ___ ___ p   h ___ y ___

s ___ ___ l   cr ___ ___   b ___ nn ___   m ___ ___ l

Read each sentence. Circle the word that completes the sentence. Write the word on the line.

1. Don't make the baby _____ .	cat cry cot
2. He likes the funny _____ .	bunny bun fun
3. Did you _____ the baby smile?	see set soap
4. Can you _____ to the baby?	wit wet wave
5. It is a good _____ .	get game gate
6. The baby is _____ to see you.	hay happy hail

Name _____

Read each sentence. Circle the word that completes the sentence. Write the word on the line.

1. Look at that _____.	bite by bee
2. It can _____ very fast.	fry fly feed
3. The hive is its _____.	home hose hay
4. It landed _____ a rose.	by bait bite
5. The bee _____ the rose.	likes lakes lines
6. The bee will fly into the _____.	soak sky sat

Old King Cole

Old King Cole was a merry old soul,
a merry old soul was he.
He called for his pipe,
and he called for his bowl,
and he called for his fiddlers three.

Nursery Rhyme

Use your own words to complete the poem.
Then draw a picture.

Old Queen Cole

Old Queen Cole was a merry old soul,
a merry old soul was she.

_____

- -

She called for her _____ ,

_____

- -

and she called for her _____ ,

_____ _____

- -

and she called for her _____ _____ .

Mike and Jane like the cute boat.

1

Mike and Jane get in line to pay.

3

fold

fold

Mike and Jane pay the lady for the boat.

4

Mike and Jane will take it home to sail.

6

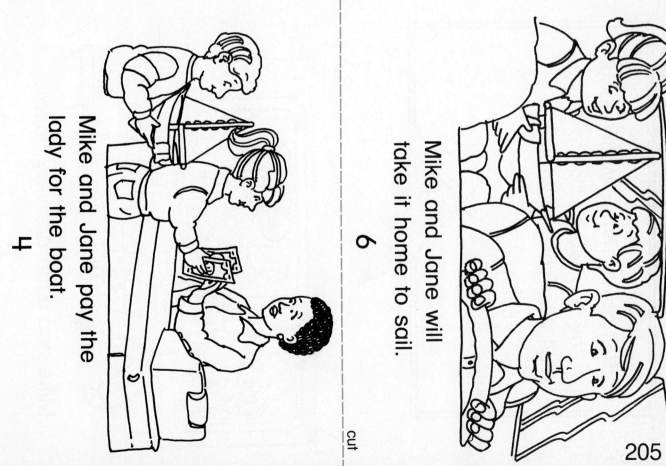

The Boat

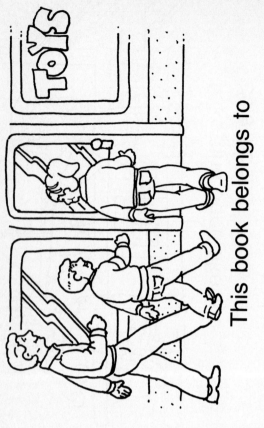

This book belongs to

Jane reads the tag.

2

Writing Activity: Write about a toy you would like to buy. Tell why you would like to buy it.

Mike and Jane are very happy.

5

Name each picture. Circle the picture name. Write the name.

can
cane
_____

kite
kit
_____

note
not
_____

wed
weed
_____

rob
robe
_____

cube
cub
_____

seat
set
_____

tub
tube
_____

pony
pot
_____

Name _____

Name each picture. Fill in the circle
next to the picture name. Write the name.

○ cone
○ cane
_____

○ bake
○ bike
_____

○ leaf
○ loaf
_____

○ bay
○ bee
_____

○ rise
○ rose
_____

○ dime
○ dome
_____

○ time
○ twenty
_____

○ cry
○ crime
_____

○ mule
○ mile
_____

○ gate
○ goat
_____

○ pail
○ pile
_____

○ hide
○ hay
_____

Name the picture. Listen to the first part of the word. Write the first two letters.

sk   sl   sm   sn   st

sm

Name _____

UNIT 4: Initial Consonant Blends with s   209

Name each picture. Circle the picture
name. Write the name.

stamp
slap
sand

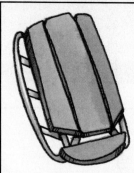

slate
sale
skate

seed
sled
skid

smoke
stake
soak

sake
snake
skate

stunk
sunk
skunk

snore
sore
stove

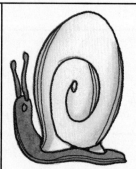

sail
stain
snail

slide
smile
side

Name the picture. Listen to the first part of the word. Write the first two letters.

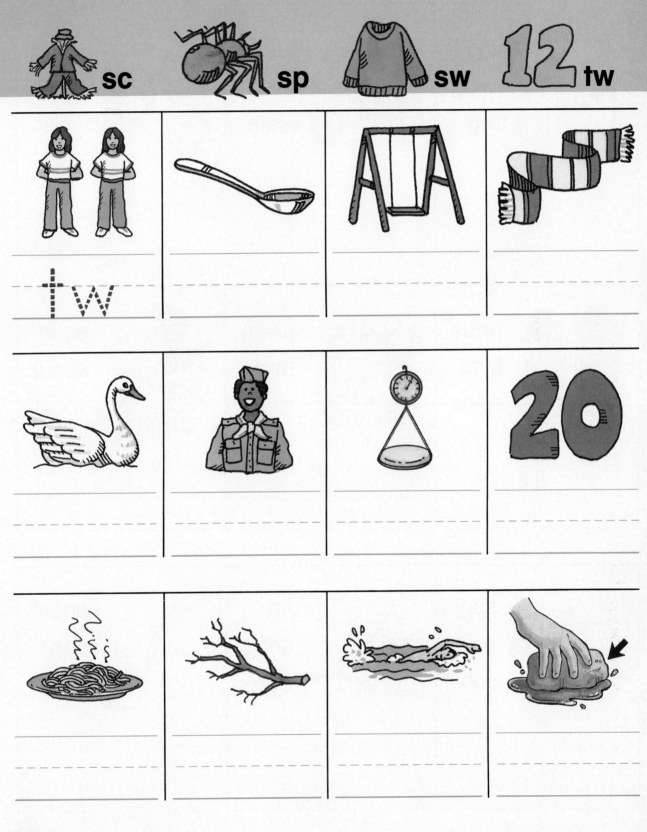

tw

Name _____

UNIT 4: Initial Consonant Blends with s and tw   211

Name each picture. Circle the picture name. Write the name.

sing swing twig	sale swam scale	spill skill sill
twins tens spins	swim twin sit	soap spout scout
spot scat sob	tip snag twig	spoon soon swoop

Name the picture. Listen to the first part of the word. Write the first two letters.

br cr dr fr

fr

Name _____

  UNIT 4: Initial Consonant Blends with r   213

Name each picture. Circle the picture name. Write the name.

bride
crime
bike
_____

brag
cab
crab
_____

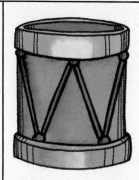
drum
bran
dug
_____

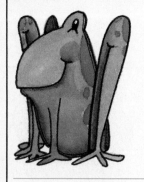
fog
frog
drop
_____

drapes
brick
back
_____

drain
brain
date
_____

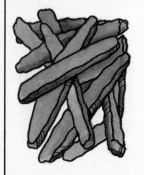
fires
cries
fries
_____

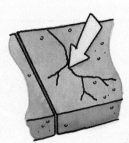
crack
free
cake
_____

crush
brush
bush
_____

Name the picture. Listen to the first part
of the word. Write the first two letters.
Color the pictures.

 **gr**    **pr**   **tr**

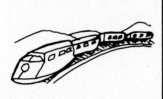

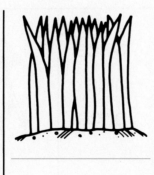

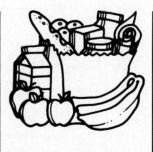

Name _____

UNIT 4: Initial Consonant Blends with r   215

Name each picture. Circle the picture name. Write the name. Color the pictures.

grapes
drapes
gates

fee
free
tree

bride
prize
pride

rain
train
brain

press
dress
mess

dress
grass
brass

gray
tray
pray

twice
nice
price

grill
drill
frill

Name the picture. Listen to the first part of the word. Write the first two letters.

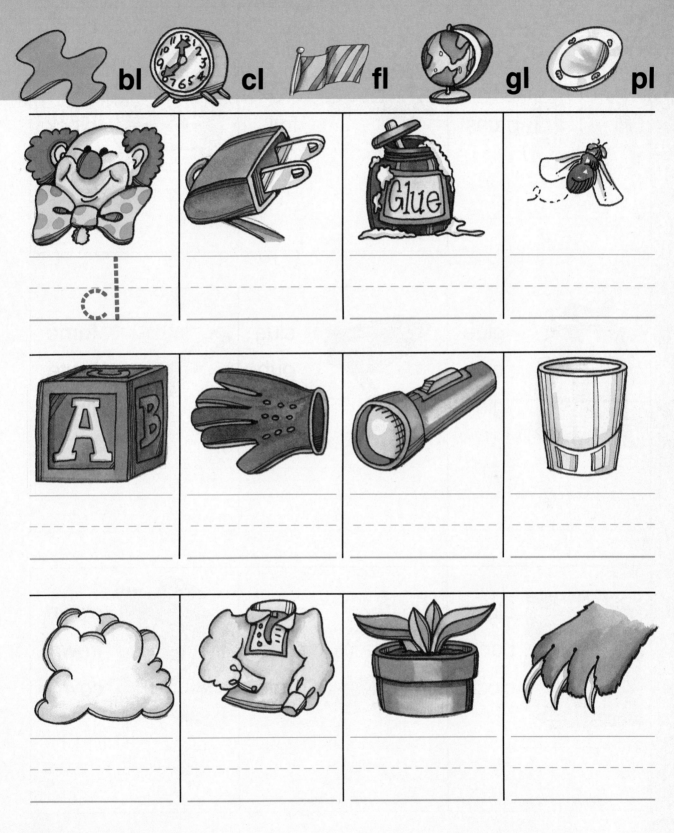

bl   cl   fl   gl   pl

cl

Name each picture. Circle the picture name. Write the name.

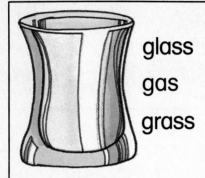

glass
gas
grass

_____

drag
flag
fall

_____

coal
clock
block

_____

glue
blue
girl

_____

slug
pup
plug

_____

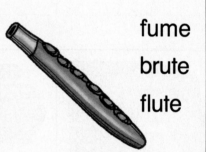

fume
brute
flute

_____

block
back
clock

_____

pale
plate
grate

_____

clown
frown
cow

_____

Read each sentence. Circle the word that completes the sentence. Write the word on the line.

1. I had a _____ .	dream gleam steam
2. It made me _____ .	snail mile smile
3. I dreamed I was in a _____ .	plane crane pane
4. It went high in the _____ .	sly sky fly
5. It made me feel so _____ .	free tree flee
6. I want to _____ in bed and dream.	clay stay tray

Name _____

Read each sentence. Circle the word that completes the sentence. Write the word on the line.

1. Let's _____ a game .		clay gray play
2. What color is a _____ ?		fog frog smog
3. I think it is _____ .		clean seen green
4. What animal is _____ ?		crack track black
5. A _____ is black .		try fly pry
6. Are any animals _____ ?		clay play gray

Name each picture. Write **ch** if you hear
the first sound in **chair.** Write **wh** if you
hear the first sound in **whale.**

ch

wh

ch

Name _____

UNIT 4: Initial Consonant Digraphs ch, wh   **221**

Name each picture. Circle the picture name. Write the name.

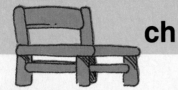 **ch**  **wh**

chin
can
when

_____
_____

chip
whip
win

_____
_____

whale
cheek
week

_____
_____

cheese
case
wheeze

_____
_____

cheap
wheel
will

_____
_____

which
chick
wick

_____
_____

cheat
wheat
weed

_____
_____

when
chest
test

_____
_____

chess
whip
dress

_____
_____

Name each picture. Write **th** if you hear
the first sound in **them** or **thumb.** Write
sh if you hear the first sound in **shoe.**

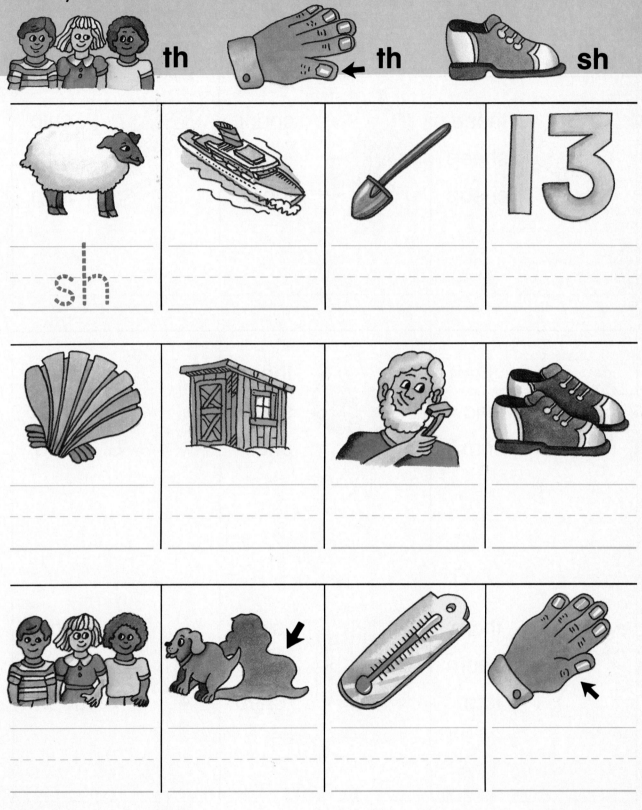

Name _____

UNIT 4: Initial Consonant Digraphs sh, th   223

Say each picture name. Circle the word that names the picture. Write the name.

 **th**    **th**    **sh**

	these sheep cheap	 spark shark thorn	 chip thin ship
	them show trim	 those spell shell	 shirt third skirt
	thorn shorn torn	 sled then shed	 thumb shut tub

Say each picture name. Listen for the
last sound. Write the name.

ch

th

moth

bea___

in___

rea___

pa___

pea___

ba___

clo___

ma___

Say each picture name. Write the name.

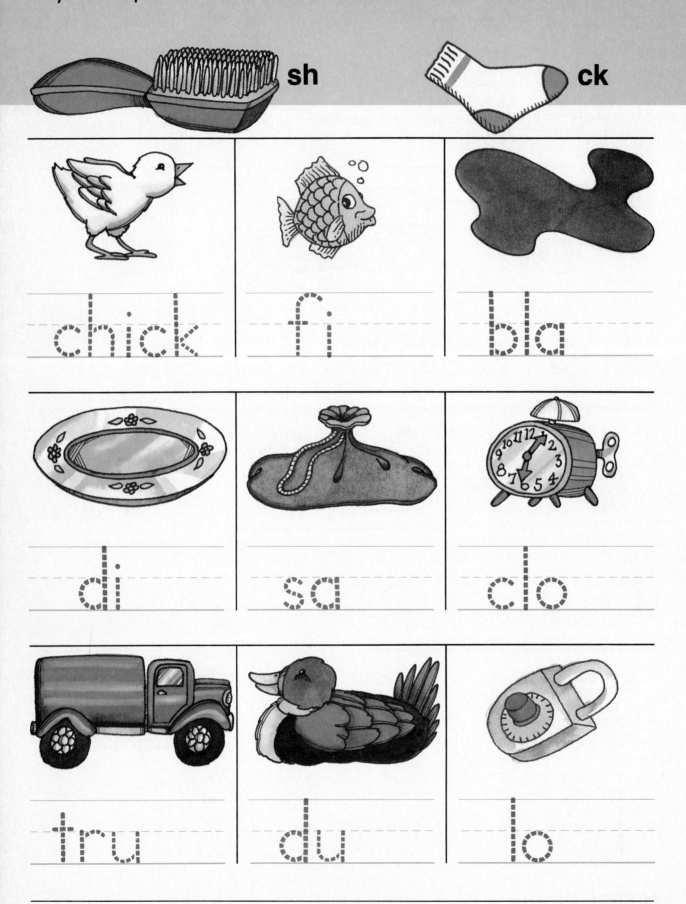

sh

ck

chick

fi___

bla___

di___

sa___

clo___

tru___

du___

lo___

Name each picture. Write **ng** if you hear the
last sound in **ring**. Write **nk** if you hear
the last sound in **sink**. Color the pictures.

 ng    **nk**

wi___   ba___   ri___   bu___

si___   ta___   si___   fa___

sku___   swi___   i___   ki___

Name _____

UNIT 4: Final Consonant Digraphs ng, nk   **227**

Name each picture. Circle the picture name. Write the name. Color the pictures.

truck
trunk
trash

_____

_____

fang
fan
frank

_____

_____

long
leash
leak

_____

_____

sock
sang
sank

_____

_____

cash
crank
couch

_____

_____

mash
mouth
much

_____

_____

drink
duck
dish

_____

_____

clink
clock
cloth

_____

_____

bang
bank
bath

_____

_____

Read each sentence. Circle the word that completes the sentence. Write the word on the line.

1. Have you ever made a _____ ?	with wish wild	
2. I _____ I will make one.	think blink chunk	
3. Will _____ wish come true?	ship this miss	
4. I wish I had a big _____ .	cheap steel wheel	
5. I need it for the _____ of my bike.	bath bring back	
6. Is a wheel _____ to get?	chest cheap cheek	

Name _____

Read each sentence. Circle the word
that completes the sentence. Write the
word on the line.

1. Jan was _____ in bed.	sick pick sink
2. Mom gave her a baby _____ .	chick thick quick
3. It had two _____ spots.	quite thing white
4. The chick had a fat _____ .	whale shape tape
5. Jan will _____ Mom.	blank thank bank
6. Mom is _____ to help Jan get well.	chick quick thick

Read each sentence. Circle the word that completes the sentence. Write the word on the line.

1. This _____ will put on a play.	trade grade blade
2. Bev will be a _____ in the play.	trunk stunk skunk
3. Lee will be a gray _____ .	whale stale scale
4. Who will be the green _____ ?	frog smog grog
5. We need a _____ , too.	grab drab crab
6. I _____ I will play the snake.	think twink drink

Name _____

Read each sentence. Circle the word that completes the sentence. Write the word on the line.

1. What games do you like to _____ ?		stay play clay
2. I like to _____ on ice.		skate plate crate
3. I ride my sled on _____ .		snow crow glow
4. I like to skip _____ on the lake.		rocks blocks clocks
5. Can you _____ of more games?		blink drink think
6. I like to _____ in the lake.		brim swim trim

Read the story. Then read the
sentences. Underline the answer.
Then write it. Color the picture.

The Snake

A black snake creeps on
the dry grains of sand.
It can twist and slide its
thick skin on the hot sand.
It thinks of sleep on a rock
at the creek.
It makes a wish for a cold, wet drink.

From the story you can tell that:

It may freeze.

It is a hot dry day.

A breeze broke the heat.

Name _____

Read more of the story. Then read the sentences. Underline the answer. Then write it. Color the picture.

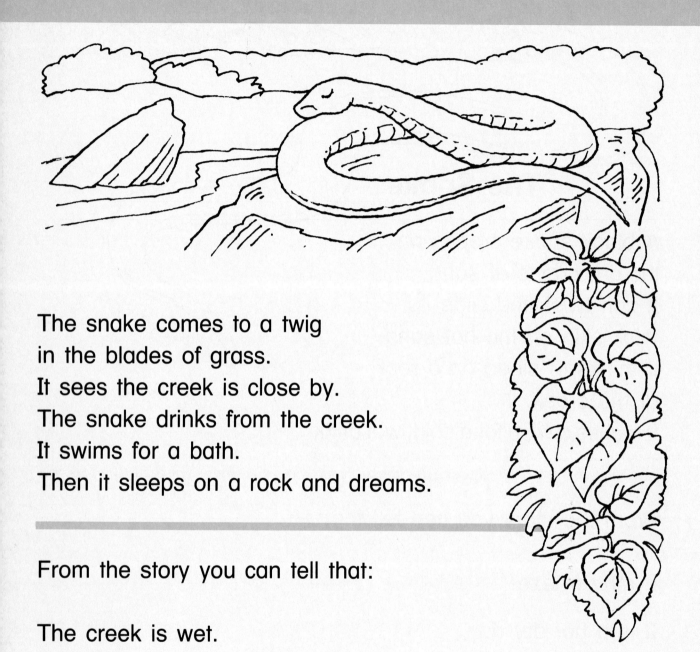

The snake comes to a twig
in the blades of grass.
It sees the creek is close by.
The snake drinks from the creek.
It swims for a bath.
Then it sleeps on a rock and dreams.

From the story you can tell that:

The creek is wet.

The creek is dry.

The creek is in a dream.

Brooms

On stormy days
When the wind is high,
Tall trees are brooms
Sweeping the sky.

They swish their branches
In buckets of rain
And swash and sweep it
Blue again.

Dorothy Aldis

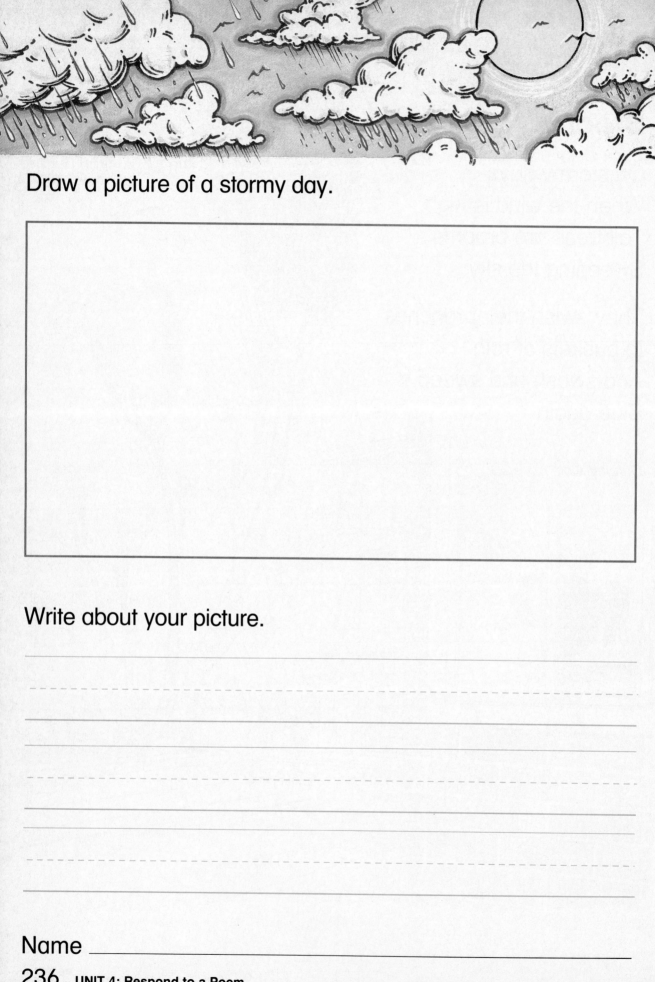

Draw a picture of a stormy day.

Write about your picture.

Name _____

Name each picture. Circle the picture name. Write the name.

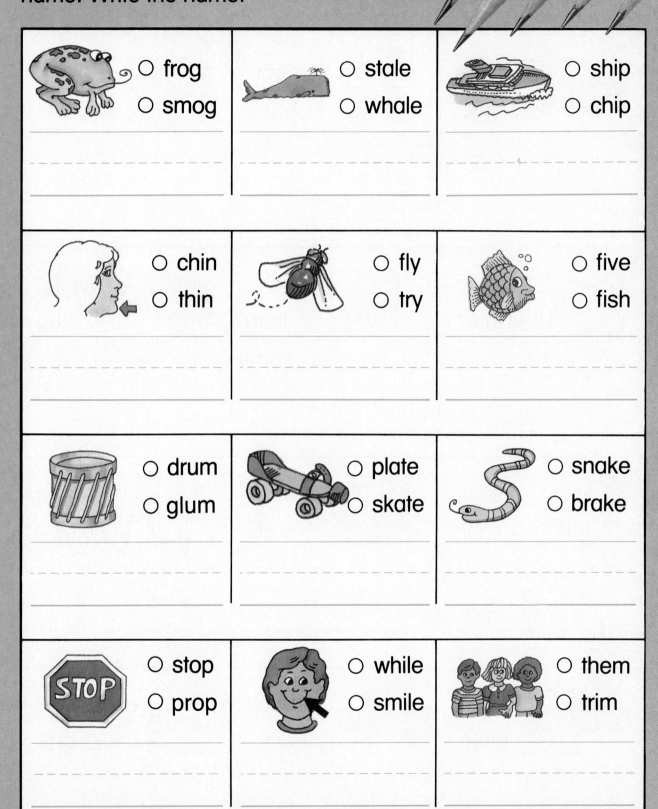

○ frog
○ smog

_____

○ stale
○ whale

_____

○ ship
○ chip

_____

○ chin
○ thin

_____

○ fly
○ try

_____

○ five
○ fish

_____

○ drum
○ glum

_____

○ plate
○ skate

_____

○ snake
○ brake

_____

○ stop
○ prop

_____

○ while
○ smile

_____

○ them
○ trim

_____

Name _____

UNIT 4: Assess Consonant Blends and Digraphs 237

Name each picture. Fill in the circle next to the picture name. Write the name.

 ○ sled
○ fled

 ○ spin
○ twins

 ○ clock
○ block

 ○ proud
○ cloud

 ○ ink
○ inch

 ○ plug
○ slug

 ○ sock
○ sash

 ○ scab
○ crab

 ○ swing
○ sink

 ○ mock
○ moth

 ○ struck
○ truck

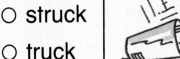 ○ spill
○ grill

Read the name. Write the word.
Add an **s** to the word if you
see more than one.

one   more than one

cat   cats

ant

ants

bee

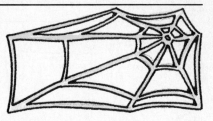

web

frog

mule

goat

bike

dog

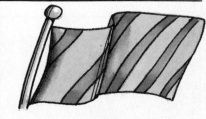

flag

Name _____

UNIT 5: Form Plurals with s 239

Add **es** to words that end in **s, ss, x, ch,** or **sh**. Read the name. Write the word. Add **es** to the word if you see more than one.

one

brush

more than one

brushes

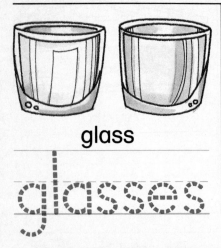

glass

gIasses

fox

_____

_____

dish

_____

_____

bus

_____

_____

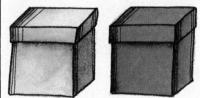

box

_____

_____

dress

_____

_____

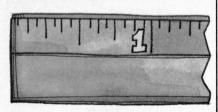

inch

_____

_____

fish

_____

_____

peach

_____

_____

Read the name. Write the word. Add **s**
or **es** to mean more than one. Add **es**
to words that end in **s, ss, x, ch,** or **sh.**

brush

dog

inch

drum

bus

hat

glass

fox

bike

six

tree

dish

Name _____

Read the two sentences. Circle the one that tells about the picture.

1. The dish is on the table.

   The dishes are on the table.

2. The box is on the shelf.

   The boxes are on the shelf.

3. The kids sit on a bench.

   The kids sit on the benches.

4. One bus is at the stop.

   Two buses are at the stop.

5. We take a cat in a box.

   We take the cats in boxes.

6. One fox sits by the cave.

   Two foxes sit by the cave.

Read the sentence. Write the word in
the next sentence. Then add **s** to make
a new word.

1. The cats <u>eat</u>. The cat _eats_ .

2. The dogs <u>jump</u>. The dog _____ .

3. The kids <u>play</u>. The kid _____ .

4. I <u>see</u> the pets. She _____ the pets.

5. Cats <u>chase</u> bugs. A cat _____ bugs.

6. I <u>get</u> a pet. He _____ a pet.

7. We <u>thank</u> a man. He _____ a man.

Name _____

Read the sentence. Write the word in the next sentence. Then add **ing** to make a new word.

1. The frogs <u>jump</u>. The frogs are _jumping_.

2. I can <u>sing</u>. I am _____.

3. A plane can <u>fly</u>. A plane is _____.

4. We will not <u>go</u>. We are not _____.

5. The dogs <u>eat</u>. The dogs are _____.

6. The kids <u>think</u>. The kids are _____.

7. The play will <u>end</u>. The play is _____.

8. We can <u>fish</u>. We are _____.

Read the sentence. Write the word
in the next sentence. Then add **ed** to
make a new word.

1. The ducks <u>quack</u>.   The ducks quacked.

2. I <u>pick</u> the weeds.   I _____ the weeds.

3. I <u>plant</u> a rose bush.   I _____ the bush.

4. I can <u>stay</u> a week.   I _____ a week.

5. I <u>fish</u> on a lake.   I _____ on a lake.

6. I <u>miss</u> my lost cat.   I _____ my cat.

7. She will <u>ask</u> you.   She _____ you.

Name _____

Read each sentence. Circle the word
that completes the sentence. Write the
word on the line.

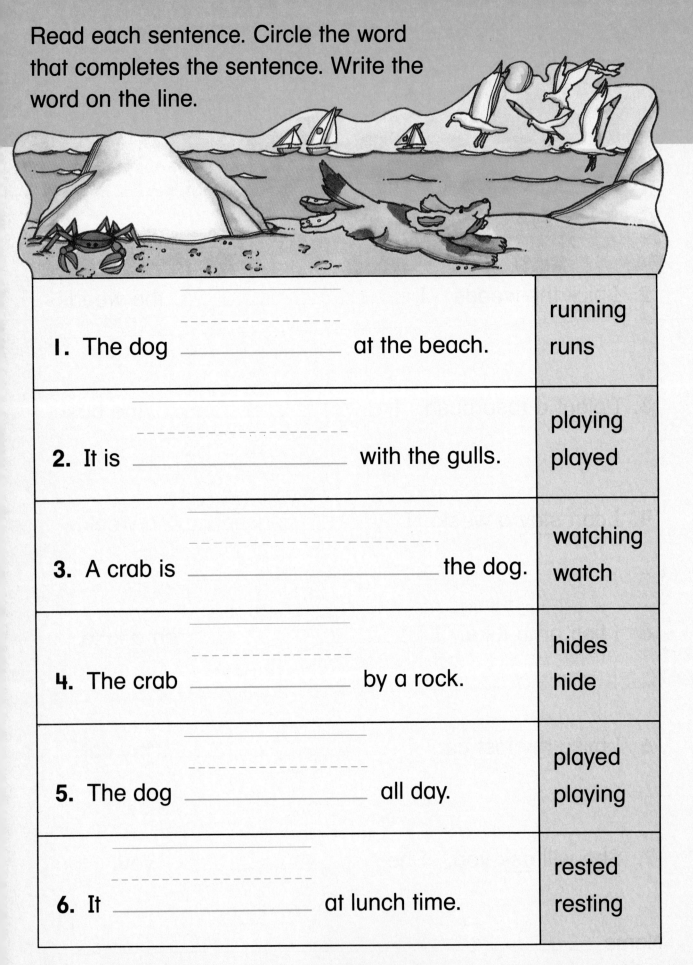

1. The dog _____ at the beach.	running runs
2. It is _____ with the gulls.	playing played
3. A crab is _____ the dog.	watching watch
4. The crab _____ by a rock.	hides hide
5. The dog _____ all day.	played playing
6. It _____ at lunch time.	rested resting

Read the story. Choose the best title.
Circle it. Then write it on the line.
Color the picture.

_____

- -

_____

Spring comes at last.
The sun shines each day.
Trees and bushes are turning green.
Spring brings flowers and warm days.
We waited for spring.
Now it is here!

All About Spring

Spring Is Here

A Wet Winter

Name _____

Read more of the story. Then read the sentences in the box.
Write the sentences that come first, next, and last.
Color the picture.

The cold winter days are over.
The snow is melted.
It is raining.
Then the rain stops and the sun comes out.
Foxes drink from the streams.
It feels like spring.

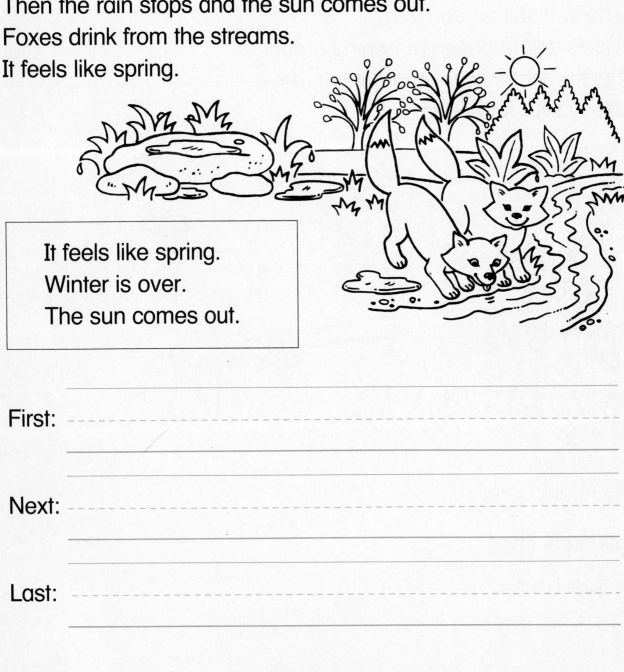

It feels like spring.
Winter is over.
The sun comes out.

First: _____

Next: _____

Last: _____

Name _____

Draw a line from the two words in color
to the one word that means the same.

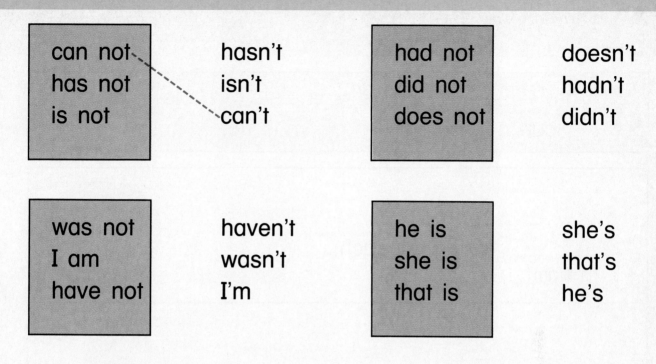

can not
has not
is not

hasn't
isn't
can't

had not
did not
does not

doesn't
hadn't
didn't

was not
I am
have not

haven't
wasn't
I'm

he is
she is
that is

she's
that's
he's

Write one word that means the same
as the two words in color.

can not	did not	I am

can't

is not	that is	have not

Name _____

Read each sentence. Write the one
word that means the same as the
two words under the line.

| I am = I'm | she is = she's | he is = he's |
| can not = can't | | has not = hasn't |

1. _____ eating a peach.
      <u>I am</u>

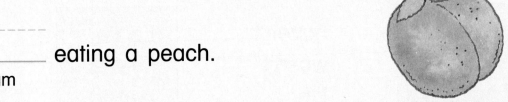

2. _____ fishing at the lake.
      <u>He is</u>

3. _____ flying a kite.
      <u>She is</u>

4. Joe _____ take his coat.
       <u>can not</u>

5. Pat _____ used the bike.
      <u>has not</u>

Say the picture name. Read the words.
Put the words together. Write the new
words. Color the pictures.

tea + cup

_____

- - - - - - - - - -

sail + boat

_____

- - - - - - - - - -

pan + cake

_____

- - - - - - - - - -

foot + ball

_____

- - - - - - - - - -

bee + hive

_____

- - - - - - - - - -

paint + brush

_____

- - - - - - - - - -

rain + coat

_____

- - - - - - - - - -

camp + fire

_____

- - - - - - - - - -

Name _____

Read the two sentences. Circle the one that tells about the picture.

1. She's up in the treetop.

She's up on the hillside.

2. The flag wasn't on the flagpole.

The flag was on the flagpole.

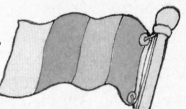

3. I did crack the eggshell.

I didn't crack the eggshell.

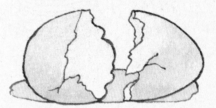

4. I wasn't sleeping at bedtime.

I wasn't reading at bedtime.

5. He hasn't seen a seashell.

He has seen a seashell.

6. The paintbrush isn't clean.

The paint isn't clean.

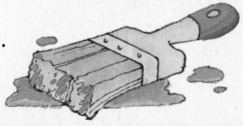

Morning Song

Today is a day to catch tadpoles.
Today is a day to explore.
Today is a day to get started.
Come on! Let's not sleep anymore.

Outside the sunbeams are dancing.
The leaves sing a rustling song.
Today is a day for adventures,
And I hope that you'll come along!

Bobbi Katz

What would you like to do tomorrow?
Complete the poem with your own words.
Then draw a picture.

Tomorrow

Tomorrow is a day to _____ .

Tomorrow is a day to _____ .

Come on, let's _____ !

cut

Beth can fly her
airplane today.

1

fold

The airplane is flying
in the sunshine.

3

So, Beth landed the
airplane by the windmill.

6

The airplane is turning
at the hillside.

4

cut

255

The Airplane

This book belongs to

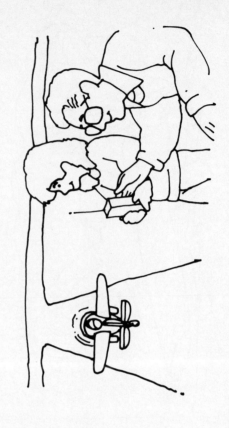

Dad helps Beth take off from the runway.

2

Writing Activity: Write a story about a trip you would take on an airplane.

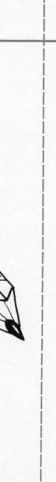

It's getting late, and Beth can't fly at sunset.

5

Read each sentence. Circle the word that
completes the sentence. Write the
word on the line.

1. I _____ see in the dark.	can't hasn't
2. A cat is _____ on the bed.	sleeps sleeping
3. You have _____ a cute pet.	picked pick
4. The cake is _____.	homemade handshake
5. A car _____ into a truck.	bumping bumped
6. _____ going to the seashore.	She's Didn't
7. It is raining _____.	outside inside

Name _____

Copyright © 1995 Steck-Vaughn Company

Read the sentence. Fill in the circle next to
the word that completes the sentence.
Write the word on the line.

1. Ben _____ take his raincoat.	○ isn't ○ didn't
2. We are _____ at the lake.	○ fishing ○ fish
3. My dog _____ when I get home.	○ jumping ○ jumps
4. The _____ has wings.	○ bathtub ○ butterfly
5. I _____ when the ball came.	○ ducked ○ duck
6. _____ outside on the porch.	○ I ○ I'm
7. Jamal made a _____ this winter.	○ snowman ○ raindrop

Look at the letter in the box.
Circle the picture whose name **begins** with the letter.

Name _____

Look at the letter in the box.
Circle the picture whose name
begins with the letter.

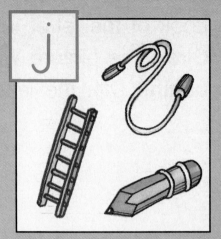

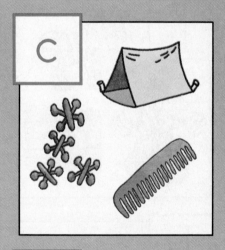

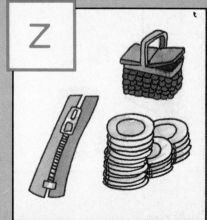

Say the picture name. Circle the letter that stands for the last sound in the picture name.

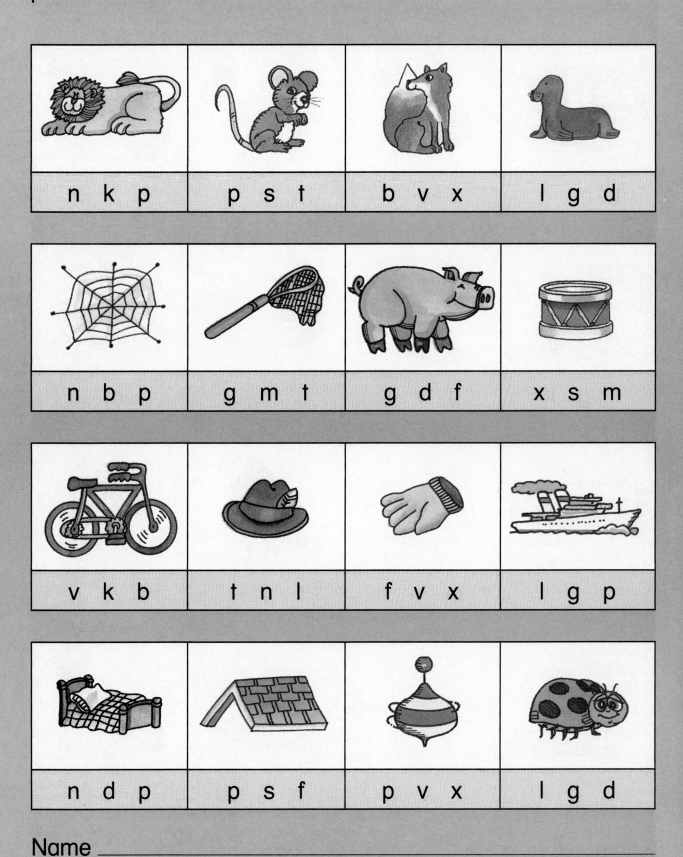

n k p

p s t

b v x

l g d

n b p

g m t

g d f

x s m

v k b

t n l

f v x

l g p

n d p

p s f

p v x

l g d

Name _____

Final Assessment of Final Consonants

Say the picture name. Circle the letter
that stands for the **middle** sound in the
picture name.

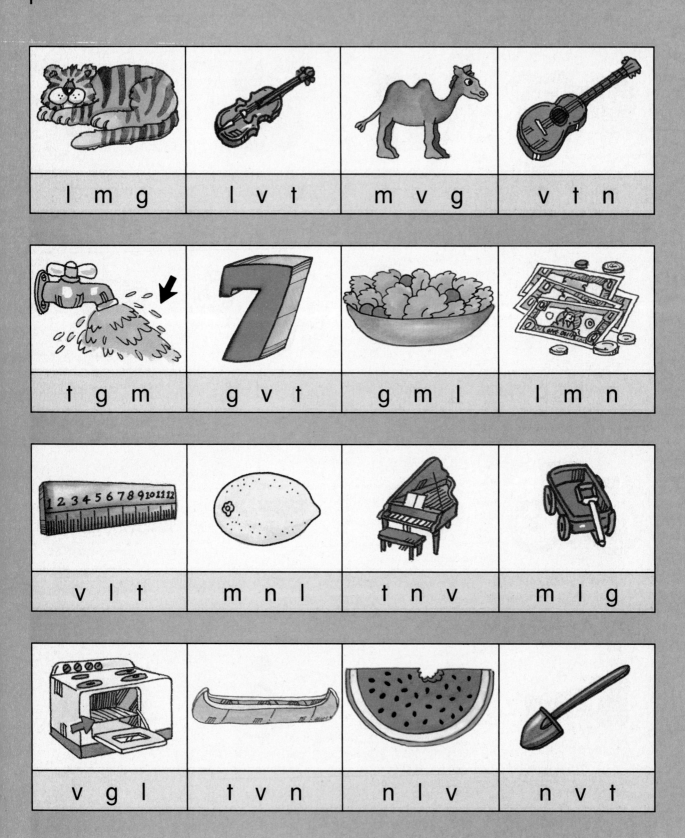

l m g   l v t   m v g   v t n

t g m   g v t   g m l   l m n

v l t   m n l   t n v   m l g

v g l   t v n   n l v   n v t

Name _____

Final Assessment of Medial Consonants

Say the picture name. Circle the **vowel**
that stands for the vowel sound in the
picture name.

a o i	a e o	u o i	a e o

a u i	o-e a-e i-e	i-e a-e o-e	a-e oa i-e

ai a i	a-e ee o-e	u-e i-e o-e	o-e u-e ea

y a-e o	i ay ea	a-e ee u-e	e y o

Name _____

Say the picture names. Circle the letters
whose sound **begins** the picture name.

wh ch sh		th wh sh		ch th sh	
th wh sh		wh ch sh		sh ch th	

Say the picture names. Circle the letters
whose sound **ends** the picture name.

	nk sh ch		sh th ch		ch nk th
	th ng nk		th sh nk		ch nk ng

Final Assessment of Consonant Digraphs

Look at the letters in the box. Circle the pictures whose names **begin** with these letters.

Name _____

Final Assessment of Initial Consonant Blends

Look at the letters in the box. Circle the pictures whose names **begin** with these letters.

pr

fr

cr

gl

sn

fl

tr

st

cl

pl

sm

Look at the picture. Read the sentences.
Fill in the circle next to the sentence
that tells about the picture.

I. ○ She has one penny.

  ○ She has one dime.

  ○ She has five dimes.

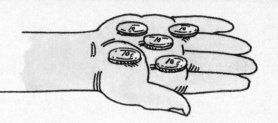

2. ○ We skate on the ice.

  ○ The cup has a hole in it.

  ○ The ice cube is in the glass.

3. ○ They sit on the rug.

  ○ They like to jog.

  ○ The men run home.

4. ○ Mike will fly a plane.

  ○ Mike will bake a cake.

  ○ Mike will ride a bike.

5. ○ A dish is on the seat.

  ○ The dish is green.

  ○ A dish fell and broke.

6. ○ The jam is on the shelf.

  ○ We will eat the beans.

  ○ We will eat the jam.

Name _____

Look at the picture. Read the sentences.
Fill in the circle next to the sentence
that tells about the picture.

1. ○ The puppy licked a cat.

○ The cat can't fix the bike.

○ A puppy jumped at a cat.

2. ○ He's sleeping on a cot.

○ An ant is sleeping in a hole.

○ She's sleeping on the grass.

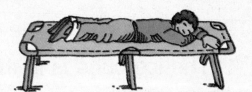

3. ○ The ants are helping to make a home.

○ The mole is fixing a home.

○ The ants are eating a cupcake.

4. ○ The foxes see a baby fox.

○ The fox sees a goldfish.

○ The fox is standing on a block.

5. ○ They see a plant by the lake.

○ They are fishing by the lake.

○ They will wade in the lake.

6. ○ The kids are flying a kite.

○ The kids are jumping rope.

○ Kids are picking the weeds.